BALI
& ISLANDS

Second Edition, 2018
Lost Guides
www.thelostguides.com

Author
Anna Chittenden

Photographer
Anna Chittenden

Editor & Proofreaders
Josie Ferguson
Camilla Lindberg Christensen
Marina Melrose

Creative Director
Sarah and Schooling

Map Illustrator
Lindsey Balbierz

Cover Image
'Balangan Beach'
by Tino Renato @tinorenato

Printed and bound in Singapore by Markono Print Media Pte Ltd

FSC
www.fsc.org
MIX
Paper from
responsible sources
FSC™ C009578

ISBN 978-981-11-4361-8

Work with Lost Guides
Lost Guides is able to deliver bespoke travel guides and custom content for your business in both print and digital formats. If you like what we do, please email *hello@thelostguides.com*

Stock this book
If you are interested in stocking *Lost Guides — Bali & Islands*, please email *hello@thelostguides.com*

Also available in this series: *Lost Guides — Singapore*

BALI
& ISLANDS

A UNIQUE, STYLISH AND OFFBEAT TRAVEL GUIDE
TO BALI AND ITS SURROUNDING ISLANDS

LOST GUIDES

2ND EDITION

ANNA CHITTENDEN

Contents

Bali

Islands

Interviews

Author's Notes

I wrote the first edition of this book in 2015. After exploring Bali on trips taken over a couple of years, I created a travel guide covering my favourite places, which has since been used by thousands of travellers from all over the world, from New York to New Caledonia, Singapore to Sweden and many places in between. Since then, I've continued exploring this fabulous part of the world, discovering Lombok and its little islands, and experiencing the wonders of the Komodo Islands, as well as digging deeper to find more unique places in Bali. I'm so happy that I can finally share all my findings with you in this new and improved book, and that you enjoy your visit to Indonesia as much as I have enjoyed creating this guide.

What's in the guide?

This book highlights over 130 of the most delightful and special spots that I have discovered during my travels around Bali, Nusa Lembongan, Lombok, Gili Islands and the Komodo Islands over the last 4 years. I've personally visited each place and have included those restaurants that I always return to, boutique hotels where I tell my friends to stay, shops where I buy my favourite outfits from, or beaches where I like to spend afternoons reading a new novel. I lugged around my DSLR camera to fill the book with original photography to give a true representation of each spot. I interviewed three fascinating people who have started creative ventures in Bali, so I hope you'll enjoy reading their stories.

How did I choose what would go in the book?

I'm naturally drawn to small and intimate places, where you might have the owner greeting you at the door, and you can feel their hard work and passion running through every aspect of the business. I love hearing a chef talk about their commitment to local sourcing or meeting an artist whose skills have been passed down through generations. I enjoy staying at places that are thoughtful and authentic, but are affordable at the same time.

All the recommendations that appear in this book are here because they are great! I haven't accepted commissions or payments to feature places in this guide – I simply write about what I love.

Who is this book for?

I have created this book for today's traveller - the stylish nomad with an interest in experience rather than expense and an eye for quality, design and authenticity. It is for those that don't require over-the-top extravagance, nor have the budget of a backpacker – but are in search of those special places in-between.

About the Author

Originally from the UK, in 2014 I packed my bags and said goodbye to London to start a new life in Asia. I live in Singapore, which is a great base from which to explore the Southeast Asia region. Coming from an outsider's perspective, I'm always on the lookout for what is unique to each specific region, be that food, art, culture, nature or everyday local life.

Lost Guides

I started my travel guide brand **Lost Guides** after becoming increasingly frustrated with trying to find trustworthy and useful travel recommendations for someone like me who's looking for authentic and unique experiences. I launched my website **thelostguides.com** with online travel guides, and have published the books: *Lost Guides – Bali* and *Lost Guides – Singapore* and now this second edition, *Lost Guides – Bali & Islands*. During 2018 I'll be spending time in Japan to carry out research for my next book *Lost Guides – Tokyo*, which will be out in 2019.

Say hello

I love to hear from my readers, and to see what you get up to during your travels.

You can reach me via social media or by email:

- ⓘ @lostguides
- 🐦 @lostguides
- 🅕 Lost Guides
- ✉ anna@thelostguides.com

Please share your lovely photos of your trip with me using the hashtag **#lostguidesbaliislands**

www.thelostguides.com

Need to Know

Accommodation: Throughout this book you'll find a selection of my favourite places to stay, ranging from boutique hotels that are great for two, to fabulous villas that are good for groups. I generally prefer to stay in villas for their space and privacy, and they often provide breakfast and organise transport so you get the benefits of a hotel too.

Visas: Bali has updated its visa policy to allow free entry to stay for up to 30 days for 140 nationalities. Passports must be valid for 6 months from the date of arrival. Please check with the Indonesian Embassy in your country for up-to-date visa information.

Money: The currency in Bali is Indonesian Rupiah – *Rp.* Be sure to take out cash in advance before you reach Bali, as the ATMs at the airport can often be out of order. There are many ATMs on the island, but they limit the amount of cash that can be withdrawn at one time. Restaurants and hotels take cards, while cafes and smaller businesses often only take cash.

SIM Cards: On arrival at Denpasar airport in Bali, you can buy a tourist SIM card with 3G/4G Internet and local calls for about Rp300k, or $22 and they will install this for you. You can find cheaper SIMs from street stalls, although getting one from airport is the quickest and easiest option.

Alcohol: Imported alcohol such as wine and spirits are taxed very highly in Indonesia, making a tropical cocktail or glass of Sauvignon blanc quite the luxury. If you fancy a tipple, remember to pick up a bottle when passing through duty-free.

Transport: The roads in Bali can be bad, and often very busy especially around peak-season. Your hotel or villa should help you with taxi transfers from the airport. Alternatively there is an 'airport taxi counter' as soon as you walk out of security that offers a fixed price to destinations around the island. *Blue Bird* are the official taxi providers in Seminyak so be sure to use them so you're not overcharged. Apps like Uber and Grab sometimes work, although they're not allowed to do pick-ups or drop-offs at certain locations, so they're a bit unreliable. Mopeds are a popular mode of transport and can be rented cheaply by the day. If there are a few of you, it makes sense to hire a driver, which works out at around $50 per day.

When to go: Bali and Indonesia in general is a great place to visit at any time of the year. It's fortunately one of those destinations where the weather can be good all year round. Peak season is July and August when families visit during the school holidays. I personally prefer to go outside these months, as otherwise I find the island too busy. November to April is officially wet season, although you can have days with bright blue skies. The tropical rains are heavy but brief.

Note: in this book, where prices are listed as $ this is USD.

10-Day Itinerary

*Experience a bit of everything with this
slightly sped-up itinerary*

Day 1 & 2
Bukit Peninsula – *Sun & Surf*

Stay on the cliff at **Mu Bungalows** (p31) in Bingin. Go for sunset
cocktails at **Ulu Cliffhouse** (p28). Start the day with a surfing lesson on
Bingin Beach (p39) and spend the afternoon splashing around on
Thomas Beach (p27). Go up to Jimbaran for dinner at **Cuca** (p41).

Day 3 & 4
Seminyak – *Shop & Eat*

Stay at the idyllic oasis The Island Houses (p76). Have an Indonesian
dinner a Merah Putih (p54) followed by drinks and dancing at Brazilian-
inspired La Favela (p59). Pick up a morning coffee from Baby Revolver
(p50) and custom-order a leather jacket from The Bali Tailor (p63). Get
a pedicure at Bodyworks (p72) and go for a healthy lunch at Watercress
(p49). Go to Canggu for evening drinks at Ji (p89).

Day 5
Balian – *Remote Retreat*

Stop-off for a night in Balian. Sleep in the rice fields at **Matekap Lodge**
(p137) and see the black-sand shoreline at **Balian Beach** (p136).

Day 6 & 7
Ubud – *Relax & Revive*

Book a room at the stylish hotel, **Como Uma Ubud** (p121). Have drinks at the **Night Rooster** (p112) followed by dinner at **Nusantara** (p109). Make your own Balinese meal during a cooking lesson at **Be Bali Stay** (p120). Drop-in for a yoga class and an Ayurvedic massage at **The Yoga Barn** (p117). Shop for tableware at **Kevala Ceramics** (p116) and fabric from **Ikat Batik** (p114). Take a half-day trip to the village of **Tampak Siring** (p130) to see **Gunung Kawi** (p131) temple and pick up a carved cow skull.

Day 8
Lombok - *Beach & Nature*

Sleep in a room decorated with Indonesian antiques at the Tugu Hotel (p160) in north Lombok. Enjoy a treatment at the spa and unwind on Sire Beach (p159).

Day 9 & 10
Gili Asahan – *Island Escape*

Take a trip to Gili Asahan Eco Lodge (p162), a rustic retreat on one of the 'secret Gilis' beside Lombok. Swim off the beach and explore the surrounding islands by boat.

Bukit Peninsula

Surfers' Spot and Bohemian Bolthole

Bukit Peninsula, or 'The Bukit' as it's known, has been a magnet for surfers since the '70s, who travelled from afar, drawn to the region's endless string of perfect Indo-waves. While nomadic surfers still descend on these shores in droves, the cliffside villages have now become a retreat for a new wave of bohemian traveller looking for a laid-back side to Bali. Located in the southernmost point of the island, The Bukit includes the hotspots **Uluwatu** – for die-hard surf fanatics, **Bingin** – with its beautiful beaches and boutique hideaways, **Balangan** – a quiet and simple surf spot, and **Jimbaran** – which has become more developed with high-end hotels but still maintains its traditional fish market.

The international crowd that come here aren't looking for smart city-style service; they are happy to spend their days perched on a surfboard, their evenings drinking Bintang beers at a ramshackled beach bar and their nights in a wooden Balinese bungalow on a cliff. For me this is what Bali is all about.

The Bukit is defined by its stunning shoreline with its craggy limestone cliffs, which tower over an azure-tinted ocean. The beaches here are how you'd imagine Bali's to be. Cream-coloured sand sweeps around the shoreline with piercing blue waters crashing on the coast. Steep cliff access means that the beaches are quiet aside from a sprinkling of cafes and local warungs. Don't miss a visit to this wonderful part of Bali – I might see you there.

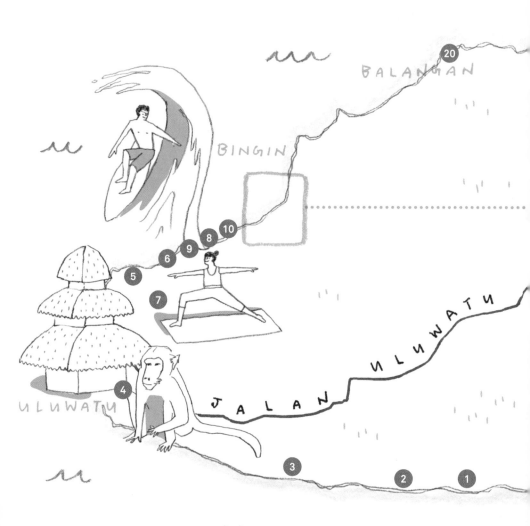

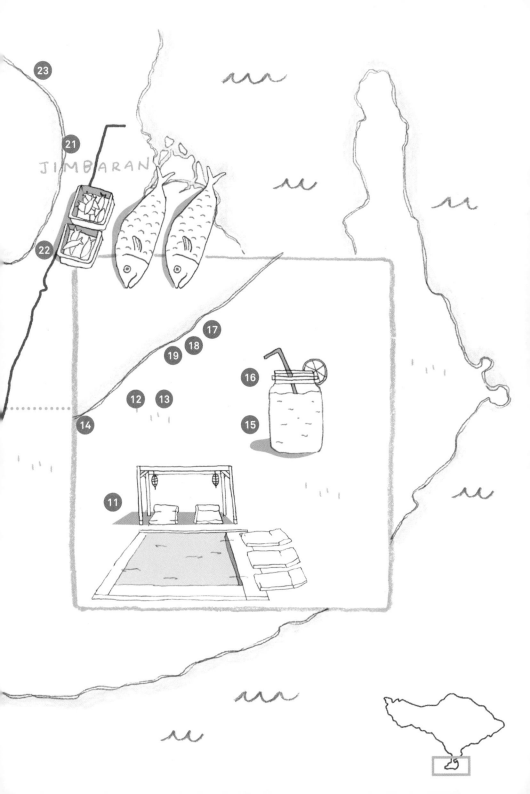

JIMBARAN

Sundays Beach Club

1 *Beautiful Beach Retreat*

It's safe to say that the south of Bali is home to many of the island's beach gems. While I'm happy enough to sip smoothies in the cafes on Bingin Beach, a trip to *Sundays Beach Club* is always a fun day out. With its rustic and relaxed Mediterranean vibe, *Sundays* hosts a private white sand beach with stunning turquoise-blue waters and an offshore coral reef. Located at *The Ungasan* resort, non-guests are also welcome and, for an entrance fee, have access to the beach club and can get involved in kayaking, snorkelling and stand-up paddle boarding. The food here is seriously tasty, ranging from grilled seafood to pizzas straight out of their stone oven. Come with a group of friends and settle in for the afternoon on the colourful beanbags with a glass of rosé in hand.

🏠 The Ungasan, Jalan Pantai Selatan Gau, Banjar Wijaya Kusum, Ungasan

☎ +62 8119421110

🔗 sundaysbeachclub.com

📷 @sundaysbeachclub

🕐 Mon - Sun 8am - 10pm

💲 Entrance fee Rp 300k (adult), Rp 50k (child), which includes Rp150k restaurant credit and water sports equipment.

The Warung at Alila Uluwatu

2 *Indo Food with a View*

If you're in The Bukit and are looking for a more luxurious sort of lunch spot as well as some great Indonesian food, or perhaps like me you enjoy nosing around a swanky hotel, then *The Warung* at *Alila Villas Uluwatu* is the place to go. *The Warung* offers traditional Indonesian cuisine with a modern twist, not to mention to-die-for views. The food is inspired by the region, so you can experience the tastes of Java, Bali and Sumatra all in one meal. The chicken and beef satays are a must, as is the 'hasil laut panggang' – Balinese grilled seafood with lobster, squid, fish and prawns. Finish off your meal with homemade ice cream, 'es krim dadar', with a coconut pancake. Their wine list is good too, which is handy to know as it can be hard to find decent wine down in this area.

🏠 Jalan Belimbing Sari, Banjar Tambiyak, Desa Pecatu

☎ +62 3618482166

↖ alilahotels.com/uluwatu

◎ @alilavillasuluwatu

⊘ Mon - Sun 11am - 11pm

Nyang Nyang Beach

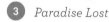

3 *Paradise Lost*

When I hear people say that Bali doesn't have any good beaches, I smile to myself and think of Nyang Nyang. You often read about 'secret beaches', which aren't actually that secret anymore. Nyang Nyang Beach, on the other hand, has managed to keep its location and identity firmly on the down-low. One reason is that it's pretty hard to find (read dirt track, fields and 500 cliffside steps). Once you get there, however, you'll be rewarded with your own little bit of paradise all to yourself. The last time I visited Nyang Nyang there was no one else there other than a few local children spearfishing in the sea. And by deserted, I mean really deserted, i.e. no drinks stalls, umbrellas or food – so bring your own supplies and shade. Good luck on your mission!

Getting There

Best done on a bike. Head towards Uluwatu Temple. You can go right towards the temple, or left – go left, past *Ulu Cafe*. Carry on another 100m until you see two white pillars just before some warungs and a launderette. Turn right down the thin pavement until the road ends. You should see a small wooden sign saying 'Nyang Nyang surf beach'. Follow the dirt track until it becomes a field with a few ruins. Walk to the end of the cliff where you will find a small drinks stall (stock up!). Make your way down the 500 steps to the beach. Enjoy!

Uluwatu Temple

4 *Spiritual Cliffside Stunner*

$ Rp50k entrance fee

Slightly south of the surf breaks at Uluwatu Beach lies the Hindu temple known locally as Pura Luhur Uluwatu. The draw here isn't so much the structure itself (Bali has more impressive temples dotted around the island), but the striking scenery. Situated on a limestone cliff 70m above the roaring ocean, it is especially beautiful at sunset. One of the oldest in Bali, this sacred sea temple was originally built in the 11th century and has links to other sea temples, such as Tanah Lot in West Bali. As this is a place of worship, make sure to cover up with appropriate clothes (they have sarongs available to borrow at the entrance). Also be aware of your belongings, as although they are said to be the protectors of the temple, there are teams of mischievous monkeys ready to snatch your bag.

Uluwatu Beach

5 *Hidden Beach at a Surfers' Paradise*

Uluwatu Beach might be one of the smallest on the island, but it could also be one of the most beautiful. With dramatic rock formations, caves and big crashing waves from the surf break, it's worth the walk down the steep cliff to check this little place out. The beach is mainly used by experienced surfers who want to reach the famous Uluwatu surf spot (Kelly Slater calls it one of the seven wonders of surf). While there isn't much opportunity for sunbathing (you're in a cave!), I like to go up to the cafe *Delphi Warung* to get the best views of the Indian Ocean while watching the surfers in action. Neighbouring Uluwatu is the swimmer-friendly Suluban Beach with stunning turquoise waters. If you're planning a visit you'll need to get your timings right though, as it's only accessible at low tide.

Getting There
When you reach the village of Uluwatu, park up and you will see cafes and bars, such as *Single Fin* at the top of the cliff. Walk down the steps until you get to Uluwatu Beach. Suluban Beach is just to the left of Uluwatu Beach.

Single Fin

6 *Surfers' Sunset Beach Bar*

Single Fin is one of those bars where you will more than likely find yourself in most evenings while staying down in The Bukit. It's a quintessential surfer's hangout with panoramic views of the famous breaks, fridges full of ice-cold Bintang beer and a huge wooden outdoor deck perched on the cliff. There's a distinctly laid-back vibe during the day, with a *Nalu Bowls* shack serving up fruit-filled acai bowls and *Revolver Espresso* for your caffeine fix. I always look forward to their 'Sunday sunset sessions' when they have a line up of live acoustic bands and DJs playing to a salty-skinned and sun-kissed crowd. Check their Facebook page for event updates, as they often have well-known acts booked in. There's also the *Single Fin* shop, which stocks some cool merchandise as well as local Bali brands.

🏠 Blue Point, Uluwatu

☎ +62 361769941

🎯 singlefinbali.com

📘 Single Fin – Bali

📷 @singlefin_bali

🕐 Mon, Tues, Thurs, Fri, Sat 10am - 10pm, Wed 10am - 12am, Sun 10am - 1am

Morning Light Yoga

7 *Ocean and Jungle View Zen*

After a morning of being battered about by waves, there's nothing better than coming to this breezy open-air yoga studio to stretch out those surf pains. Surrounded by lush foliage and situated high enough to enjoy views of the ocean, this traditional wooden-thatched hut is blissfully serene. Drop-in classes teaching Vinyasa Flow are held every day at 7.30am, 10.30am and 5.30pm and are open to all levels of experience: just arrive a few minutes before the class starts. I, for one, find the sessions particularly challenging, but they do give you a great workout and you'll see improvements after a few days. You'll find the studio located in the peaceful grounds of the lovely *Uluwatu Surf Villas*.

🏠 Uluwatu Surf Villas, Jalan Pantai Suluban, Uluwatu

☎ +62 817555421

↖ uluwatusurfvillas.com/yoga

f Morning Light Yoga Bali

◎ @morninglightyoga

⊘ Mon - Sun 7.30am, 10.30am and 5.30pm

$ Rp100k per class

Thomas Beach

8 *Off-the-beaten-path Paradise*

🏠 Jalan Labuan Sait,
Padang Padang

This beach has managed to keep itself a well-guarded secret, with only the most curious of travellers venturing down the path to one of Bali's most beautiful beaches. To find this gem, head to *Suka Espresso* and follow the dirt track opposite the cafe, which takes you to a small car park. From here, take 175 steps down (it's not as bad as it sounds!). You'll arrive at a long, sprawling beach flanked by willowy palm trees. The piercing blue water is calm and perfect for swimming and there's a long stretch of sand so it never feels too crowded. The surf here is small (so better for beginners) and there are boards for hire on the shore. Pitch up at one of the many sun loungers dotted on the beach and sip on freshly picked coconuts and cold beers. Keep in mind that this is a local spot with a few warungs and stalls for lunch and snacks, but this only adds to the charm.

Ulu Cliffhouse

9 *Beautiful Clifftop Beachclub*

This stunning area in Bali has been crying out for a stylish beach club for a while, and *Ulu Cliffhouse* has finally met the demand. The views here are absolutely enthralling – perch on a blue and white-striped sun lounger with a 'son of a beach' cocktail (gin, pomello and rosemary) in hand and gaze at the gorgeous turquoise sea ahead. Clearly, a lot of thought has gone into this place, from the cool, modern design of the space, to the tasty food and fun drinks. The vibe is friendly and relaxed and they don't try and make it feel too 'exclusive'. Food is served all day, with items such as shrimp and avocado ceviche, burgers and small pizzas as well as creative cocktail menu delights such as spiced mango daiquiri and watermelon and mint margarita, making it a perfect spot for sunset. Daybeds can be booked in advanced online – sign me up!

🏠 Jalan Labuan Sait, 315
Padang Padang

☎ +62 81338812502

↖ ulucliffhouse.com

✉ info@ulucliffhouse.com

f Ulu Cliffhouse

⌾ @ulucliffhouse

⌚ Mon – Sun 12pm – 10pm

Padang Padang Beach

10 *Sand, Swim and Surf*

A quiet and secluded beach ten minutes north from rough and ready Uluwatu Beach, Padang Padang is the perfect place to relax and take in the glorious Bukit coastline. I suggest coming here early in the morning for a swim when you can enjoy this stunning bit of sand and sea all to yourself. Not all beaches in Bali are suitable for swimming so this is a great spot. Padang Padang is also a good place to learn to surf, compared to somewhere like Kuta, which is packed with surf schools. There are plenty of local teachers around, or you can hire a board from the beach if you've already got some surf skills. On Padang Padang Beach you'll find simple warungs serving nasi goreng and refreshing drinks, and look out for the colourful boat yard where they dismantle the fishing boats every time they take them out of the sea.

Getting There
Look out for places such as *Pinkcoco Bali Hotel* and the *ilovebali* clothes shop – you are in Padang Padang. Carry on until you see signs for the beach. There are normally lots of motorbikes parked at the top. Note: you will need to walk down some steep steps to get down to the beach.

Sal Secret Spot

11 *Whitewashed Wonderland*

🏠 Jalan Pantai Bingin

☎ +62 81238942686

🏃 salbalihotel.com

✉ sal.bungalows@outlook.com

💲 From $65

The most heavenly hideaway. It was tempting to abide by its namesake and keep this place a secret, but it's just too good not to share. Set up by a Portuguese guy who moved to Bali for the surf (don't they all!), *Sal* is affordable and intimate with only ten rooms. With whitewashed walls, outdoor bathrooms and a perfect pool, it feels like a Mediterranean retreat nestled in the village of Bingin. You can choose between a cliffside room with panoramic views over the Bukit surf, or a bungalow by the pool. For breakfast they put on a spread of fresh fruit and cooked eggs, and for afternoon poolside lounging you can order jugs of Sangria. There's a cabana for massages and large Balinese daybeds can be found dotted under palm trees (the perfect spot to leaf through your book). *Sal* is a great place to stay if you're travelling solo, as the small resort is very friendly, or if you're looking for a reasonably priced guesthouse with a good friend.

Mu Bungalows

(12) *Secluded Cliffside Resort*

The views at *Mu* are mesmerising. With its prime location perched on the cliff above Bingin Beach, you can lose whole afternoons watching the sun glistening on the tips of the lapping waves. The resort has a Robinson Crusoe vibe with bungalows created using recycled and natural materials, such as beds made from bamboo and lights crafted from large seashells. You'll likely swing into an idyllic routine at *Mu*. Start the day with a breakfast of homemade bread and brioche baked fresh from the onsite bakery, with dollops of homemade jam. Then, join the daily yoga-classes in the open-air pavilion for some serious pre-surf stretches. Afterwards, wander down to Bingin Beach and dive into the surf or have a salty swim. Later, book a relaxing massage, made even more tranquil with the soothing sound of waves. Dinner at *Mu* is community-style, so you can chat to fellow travellers over delicious homemade Indonesian and Mediterranean cuisine.

🏠 Jalan Pantai Bingin

☎ +62 3618957442

↖ mu-bali.com

✉ info@mu-bali.com

f Mu Bungalows

⊙ @mu_bali

$ From $130

The Temple Lodge

13 *Bohemian Surf and Yoga Retreat*

High above the cliffs of Bingin is the super-chic surf and yoga retreat *The Temple Lodge*. Seven suites have been lovingly designed using local natural materials with colourful carved wood and traditional thatched roofs. The rooms are open-air in style, so you can feel truly at one with nature while falling asleep to the sound of the waves crashing below. Geared towards a healthy lifestyle, there are daily yoga classes, a vegetarian menu and the spoiling *Temple Spa*. The 'Temple Suite' has its own private swimming pool and huge living space, while the other rooms share a lovely cliffside infinity pool. Spend your days relaxing at the retreat or head down to the beach at Bingin for a swim, sunbathe and surf session. Non-guests can also enjoy the yoga studio or book in for a meal at the restaurant.

🏠 Jalan Pantai Bingin

☎ +62 85739011572

↖ thetemplelodge.com

✉ thetemplelodge@outlook.com

$ From $70

Impossible House

14 *Stylish Surfside Abode*

This holiday house would suit the most adventurous of souls, or perhaps those looking to recreate scenes from the film 'Swiss Family Robinson'. Subtly built into the cliff on the far end of Bingin Beach in front of Impossibles surf break, this authentic but stylishly decorated house immerses you in the raw and natural beauty of this part of Bali. It's crazy to think that you are only 45 minutes from the airport and an hour from Seminyak – it's truly another world here. You are in and amongst the environment, sandwiched between heavy rock formations and waves crashing meters from the house. Comfortably rustic, the house is designed with special attention to detail, but really it's all about the surroundings and remoteness here (there's no wifi, TV or phone signal!). Impossible House is perfect for a family or group of friends, and especially for the surf and swim obsessed as you can do both from the doorstep. Good for groups of 6-8 people, there are three private bedrooms; the top one has a terrific terrace, and there's another room positioned on a rock for front-seat sea views!

🏠 Jalan Tanjung Simah, Bingin

🏹 theislandhouses.com

✉ bookings@theislandhouses.com

📷 @theislandhouses

💲 From $350

Bingin Cafes

15 *Breakfast Spots in the Bukit*

The Cashew Tree

Located up in Bingin village, *The Cashew Tree* is a casual cafe in a relaxing garden with lazy loungers, beanbags and wooden cabanas. They pride themselves on using as many organic and local products as possible, serving up super healthy meals, such as pumpkin tofu cashew curry, spicy Asian chicken salad and my favourite, the raw cacao dessert. Be sure to stick around for their weekly 'Thursday Sessions' when live bands play and pretty much everyone in the village comes to dance the night away.

 Jalan Pantai Bingin, 9

 Mon – Sun 8am – 10pm

Drifter

There's a great cafe located at the back of the surf and lifestyle store *Drifter*. Tuck into a BBB, 'Bingin Breakfast Burrito' with scrambled eggs and guac after an active morning in the surf. For lunch they do dishes like fish tacos and vegan jackfruit tacos, as well as lots of healthy drinks like kombucha and cold press juices. The shop is pretty good too!

 Jalan Labuansait, 52

 Mon – Sun 8am – 3pm

Bukit Cafe

Located just before the turning to Bingin on the road to Padang Padang, *Bukit Cafe* is a chilled out spot serving all day brunch food. Order a fruity smoothie bowl, or fill up on pulled-pork eggs Florentine.

 Jalan Labuansait

 Mon – Sun 7am – 10pm

Suka Espresso

Converted from a roadside warung near Uluwatu, *Suka Espresso* has become a popular hangout for the young and hip surf crowd. A small open-air coffee and breakfast spot, it has items like 'Turkish bowl' with kale, quinoa and egg, and filling cheesy bagels. They also have an evening menu with portobello burgers and BBQ pork ribs.

 Jalan Labuansait, 10

 Mon – Sun 8am – 10pm

Acacia Bungalows

16 *Spacious and Serene Hideaway*

If you're looking for the space and privacy of a villa, but with the benefit of helpful staff, then look no further than *Acacia Bungalows*. Managed by the same people as *Mick's Place*, *Acacia* is similar in style, but each of its bungalows also benefit from having their own private entrance, garden and swimming pool. Staff are discreetly on hand to make you breakfast and to help with anything you need – be it a taxi, surf lessons or a spa booking. As well as the private pool, my favourite part is the huge outdoor bathrooms where you can indulge in an open-air shower under a canopy of pink bougainvillea flowers. Spa treatments and massages can be arranged at the bungalow, so you can have a pedicure whist reading on a sun lounger next to the pool – spoiling!

🏠 Jalan Pantai Bingin

☎ +61 755363325

↖ baliretreats.com.au/acacia

✉ info@baliretreats.com.au

$ From $107

Mick's Place

17 *Breathtaking Boutique Bolthole*

Who needs a big, brash, soulless hotel when you can stay at this charming cliffside hideaway? *Mick's Place* is my favourite type of accommodation – 'laid-back luxury' featuring wooden tree houses and Polynesian-style bungalows. The wow factor is the location; *Mick's Place* is uniquely situated right on top of the cliff looking down over the surf at Bingin Beach. There's a small infinity plunge pool, the perfect place to chill out with a cocktail, and be sure to book yourself in for a massage at the 'spa with a view'. The best room is the 'Honeymoon Bungalow', which has its own private pool, garden, daybeds and an indoor-outdoor bathroom – ideal for a romantic escape. Also a popular place for weddings, check out their insta @micksplacebali for the dreamiest 'take me here now' photos. Note, *Mick's Place* is adults-only, taking guests over 12 years old.

🏠 Jalan Pantai Bingin

☎ +61 755363325

↖ baliretreats.com.au/micksplace

✉ info@baliretreats.com.au

📷 @micksplacebali

💲 From $94

Kelly's Warung

18 *Barefoot Beach Shack*

Located directly on Bingin Beach, *Kelly's* is the go-to place for a post-yoga or post-surf refuel. Run by the same crew as *The Cashew Tree*, the menu is healthy but hearty, serving up pink pitaya fruit bowls, raw vegetable wraps and refreshing juices. Grab a seat on the wooden deck at *Kelly's* for wonderful panoramic views over the beach, and watch the surfers at play in the ocean in front of you. The vibe is super friendly so you'll probably end up making a few new pals while you're here. Surfers from Brazil, families from Norway, locals from Uluwatu — it's a lovely mix of people who all appreciate the simple things in life. *Kelly's* also provides cheap and cheerful accommodation above the cafe - perfect for beach bums who like to roll straight out of bed and onto the sand.

🏠 Bingin Beach

📘 Kellys Warung

📷 @kellyswarung

Bingin Beach

19 *Beautiful Bukit Beach*

This has to be one of my favourite beaches in Bali. Not only because it has soft white sand, crystal turquoise waters and a lack of crowds, but also because Bingin is one of those friendly, unpretentious places where travellers come and chat over dragon fruit smoothies at *Kelly's Warung*, or trade travel secrets while sitting on their surf boards waiting for a wave. The beach is at the bottom of a steep limestone cliff, which you access via stone steps. There are dozens of wooden thatched huts and a few simple villas to rent, all with amazing ocean views. As well as being a good swimming spot, Bingin is a good place to come for a surf and is suitable for all ranges of experience. If, like me, you prefer to go with a guide, there are lots of teachers located on the beach who can take you out for a morning surf. Come evening, Bingin Beach hosts seafood BBQs and bonfires. Bliss!

Getting There
Make your way to Bingin village. Once there, follow signs to the beach.
Note: the beach is about a seven-minute walk down some steep steps.

Balangan Beach

20 *Simple and Unspoilt Beach*

This coastal stretch has long been a favourite with surfers drawn to its reef break, but for those looking for a laid-back beach day, Balangan should also be top of your list. Somehow this beautiful, palm-fringed gem has managed to stay under-the-radar. Host to only a handful of local warungs in wooden shacks serving up snacks of nasi goreng and Bintang beer, it makes a change to the international beach-club scene of Seminyak. Swimmers can enjoy the waters when the sea is at high tide, and for those that want to laze around, the beach is lined with sun loungers and umbrellas, which can be rented for Rp50k for the day. It's worth a trip to Balangan just to see its breathtaking scenery, which is especially magical at sunset.

Getting There

Balangan Beach is easily accessible compared to the other cliffside beaches of The Bukit. Drive to Balangan village, and leave your car or bike in the car park. It's a short walk from there.

Cuca

21 *Innovative Cocktails and Culinary Creations*

🏠 Jalan Yoga Perkanthi,
Jimbaran

☎ +62 361708066

↖ cucaflavor.com

✉ service@cucaflavor.com

f Cuca

📷 @cucaflavor

I first heard whispers of *Cuca* from a mixologist at one of my favourite bars in Singapore; word of mouth recommendations from industry insiders often lead me to the best finds. Head Chef Kevin Cherkas picked up his trade from working at Michelin-starred restaurants, such as *El Bulli* in Spain, and he now runs this fab dining venue with his wife Virginia in the coconut groves of Jimbaran. Start your evening off at their alfresco bar; the cocktails are creations in themselves – think fruity alcoholic ice-lollies balanced artfully on glasses. The food is tapas-style sharing dishes divided into three categories: 'harvested' – vegetables, 'hooked' – seafood, and 'farmed' – meat. The small plates mean that you have a good excuse to order whatever you like off the menu. Just don't get too full for dessert.

Jimbaran Fish Market

22 *Barefoot Beachside Dining*

Jimbaran Bay has traditionally been a fishing village where many of Bali's restaurants come to get their supplies. While the area now features many large resorts, there's still a distinctly local feel on the beach where you'll find clusters of colourful wooden fishing boats and fishermen hauling in their catch of the day. If you come in the morning you can visit the bustling wet market, where locals set up stands selling their produce. Around sunset, the beach glows with romantic candle-lit tables while diners select from the day's fresh catch, such as live crab, lobster and fish, to be grilled for their dinner. Enjoy the sea breeze, bury your feet in the sand and eat like a king. The prices are reasonable too.

🏠 Jimbaran Bay, Jalan Bukit Permai, next to the InterContinental Resort

Jimbaran Market

23 *Lively Local Hangout*

A small market serving the local Jimbaran community, come here to see Balinese women selling their wares, such as baskets of green limes, beans and courgettes, with bright, fragrant flowers scattered all over the roadside. The laughing ladies gossip beside bowls of shiny, red apples and buckets containing pale-blue hydrangea flowers. I'm personally fascinated with the beautiful offerings nestled in palm leaf baskets, known as 'canang sari'. The Balinese people laboriously assemble these each morning from petals, and you can see them being made here. Even though it's near the tourist hotspots, it's nice to see a more local side to Bali that's often hidden. Pop by for a quick stop on your way to *Jimbaran fish market* and pick up a handful of fruit for your journey.

 Find this market towards the northern part of Jimbaran Bay, on Jalan Pantai Kedonganan.

Seminyak

Stylish Shopping and Fabulous Food

Known as the most happening place in Bali, Seminyak has grown up from being a small village populated by the island's expats, to one of the most stylish spots in Southeast Asia. Set beside a soft sandy beach with tall crashing waves, Seminyak is a unique town heavily influenced by the Australian and European inhabitants who have made Bali their home. The vibe is totally international – you'll find a French restaurant opposite an Argentinian BBQ warehouse, all against the backdrop of peaceful paddy fields under Bali's bright blue skies.

One of the most exciting sides to Seminyak is the food. World-class chefs who've tired of city life have hopped over to the shores of Bali, enticed by the beach lifestyle as well as the fantastic local produce. Enjoy innovative Asian food with a twist or fancy European fare without the hefty price tag. If you're looking for a party, you'll find boisterous beach clubs and bustling bars dotted all around town.

If you want to stock up your summer wardrobe, you have come to the right place. The shopping in Seminyak is superb. You've got designers from across the globe working with talented Balinese artisans to produce high-quality clothing and accessories, many of which are handmade, and at affordable prices.

It must be noted that as the town has become more developed, the streets are busy and the traffic is heavy. I often prefer to find a villa slightly outside of Seminyak so as to get some peace and quiet away from the hustle and bustle.

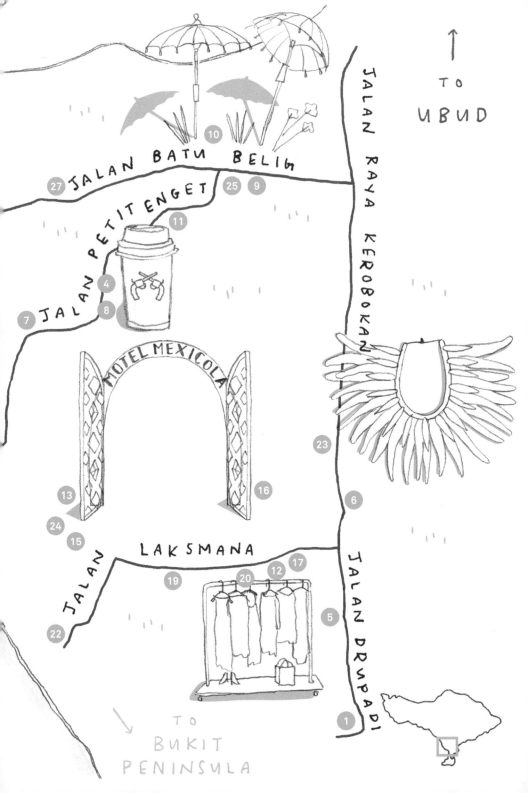

Nalu Bowls

1 *Fruity Surfers' Breakfasts*

🏠 Jalan Drupadi, 1 2A

☎ +62 81236609776

🔖 nalubowls.com

📘 Nalu Bowls

📷 @nalubowls

🕐 Mon - Sun 7.30am - 6pm

Taking inspiration from Hawaii where acai bowls are all the rage, *Nalu* (meaning 'wave' in Hawaiian) was set up to fill that smoothie-shaped hole in Seminyak's snack scene. What looks like nothing more than a whitewashed shack made of driftwood, *Nalu Bowls* cheerfully churns out stacks of coconut shells filled with blended fruit to happy and hippie customers. Each bowl is lovingly named after the owners' favourite waves from around the world. My go-to flavour is the 'Uluwatu' – filled with dragon fruit, banana, mango and raspberry. Hidden away down a narrow road off Jalan Seminyak, this place is sought out by those in the know, often by bike with a surfboard in tow. They also have sister sites at *Single Fin* down in Uluwatu and at Echo Beach in Canggu catering to the hungry surfers.

Watercress

(2) *Fresh, Organic Breakfasts*

With a focus on fresh, seasonal ingredients and inspiring flavours, this quiet and casual cafe has become a firm favourite with those looking for a healthy food fill. I like coming here for what they call their 'rustic breakfast', with options such as 'salmon & the rye', with avocado, pesto and cream cheese, or the 'Watercress omelette', with organic asparagus and zesty lemon crème fraîche. It's not all strictly healthy though, *Watercress* brings in freshly made cakes and croissants from bakery *Monsieur Spoon*, and you can get your caffeine fix here from Bali's own *Revolver Espresso*. Useful to note is that *Watercress* has parking facilities, unlike many of the cafes and restaurants in central Seminyak. If you're up in Ubud, *Watercress* also has a branch located centrally on Jalan Monkey Forest.

🏠 Jalan Batu Belig, 21a

☎ +62 85102808030

🏹 watercressbali.com

✉ info@watercressbali.com

f Watercress cafe

◎ @watercressbali

⊘ Mon – Sat 7.30am – 4pm and 6pm – 12am, Sun 7.30am – 5pm

Baby Revolver

3 *Hip Coffee Hideaway*

🏠 Jalan Petitenget, 102

☎ +62 85102444468

🔦 revolverespresso.com

✉ info@revolverespresso.com

📘 Revolver Espresso

📷 @revolverespresso

🕐 Mon - Sun 7am - 6pm

While a *Starbucks* cup was a fashion accessory for New Yorkers in the noughties, a *Revolver* cup isn't far off this for a Seminyak scenester worth their salt. The younger sister of the popular *Revolver Espresso* near Seminyak Square, 'Baby Revs' is a little hole-in-the-wall boutique coffee house providing a haven for hipster caffeine lovers. With only eight seats, the retro styled interior is pretty cosy, but its location up on quiet Jalan Petitenget means that you'll normally find a space to squeeze in. *Revolver Espresso* is considered by many to be the best coffee in Bali, and you'll see it being served at other hip hangouts like *Single Fin* and *Watercress*. As well as coffee, they do a mean all-day breakfast menu with indulgent dishes such as 'Smoking Barrel' with chili scrambled eggs, crispy bacon and feta and my go-to, 'The Assasin', a wrap with bacon, eggs, avocado, cheese and BBQ sauce.

La Lucciola

④ *Breezy Beachfront Dining*

One of Seminyak's most lovely beachside lunch locations, the Italian inspired *La Lucciola* has been around for a while and is a popular pick with returning visitors to the island. This is seaside dining like it should be: palm trees swaying in the wind, waves lapping on the shore and a stretch of golden sandy beach right in front of the restaurant. Housed in an open-air structure with a thatched roof and bamboo chairs, there's a cool ocean breeze that circulates around the building. The service is excellent, the staff super friendly and the prices are surprisingly reasonable. They're known for their tasty Italian pastas as well as fresh fish and the most refreshing fruit juices. *La Lucciola* is more of a daytime eating spot (due to its view), although it's also lovely for a cocktail or two come sunset.

🏠 Jalan Petitenget (next to Petitenget Temple)

☎ +62 361730838

🕐 Mon - Sun 9am - 11pm

Kilo

(5) *Laid-back Lounge*

🏠 Jalan Drupadi, 22

☎ +62 3614741006

🖈 kilokitchen.com/bali

✉ bali@kilokitchen.com

⊙ @kilobali

🕐 Mon - Sun 8am - 3pm,
6pm - 12am

After establishing itself as a local favourite in Singapore, the cool and casual restaurant *Kilo* has hopped over the shores and landed in this delightfully-designed minimalist building sitting discreetly along Jalan Drupadi. The vibe is very Californian; think industrial meets desert with bold concrete walls and cactuses strewn on jazzy Aztec carpets. The *Kilo* concept encourages its guests to share, which is great as you'll have a hard time choosing between delicious dishes such as wasabi tuna tartare, salt baked snapper and the 24-hour pork belly. They've now opened up for brunch too, serving tasty Asian-fusion dishes such as BBQ pork bahn mi and duck tacos, as well as comfort foods like Kilo's big breakfast and Spanish Omelette.

Mama San

6 *Stylish Asian Street Food*

For those of you that have had the pleasure of travelling and eating your way around Asia, you will know that the heart of any Asian country's food scene lies in its street food. Chef Will Meyrick brings a new twist to the Bali restaurant line up by serving innovative and fun dishes inspired by his travels, such as Vietnamese pork belly, crispy salmon with green mango, Thai beef salad and Bagan chicken curry. Set in a trendy former 'gudang', or warehouse, the design of the restaurant has a feel of a 1920's colonial gentlemen's club, with marble top mah-jong tables and oversized tan leather chesterfields. A handy tip to know is that, while the main dining room downstairs is often pre-booked, you can turn up and eat upstairs in the comfy cocktail lounge where reservations aren't required.

🏠 Jalan Raya Kerobokan, 135

☎ +62 361730436

➤ mamasanbali.com

✉ info@mamasanbali.com

📘 MamaSan Bali

📷 @mamasanbali

🕐 Mon - Sun 12pm - 3pm,
6pm - 11pm

Merah Putih

7 *Fantastic Indonesian Fare*

If I land in Bali and can get out of the airport in time for dinner, I'll often race to *Merah Putih* for that first taste of Indonesian cuisine. Begin your evening at their snazzy bar and order a refreshing cucumber and mint martini. If you are with a group of friends, book a table in one of the cosy teak pods on the mezzanine, looking over the beautifully designed restaurant. The food on the menu, split into 'traditional' and 'modern', is a great way to understand more about the local cuisine from Bali as well as other Indo islands. It's hard to pick the best dish, but for starters I like the Bakwan Kepiting (soft-shell crab fritter), the Javanese beef shank steamed buns, and the coconut smoked yellowfin tuna. For mains go for the Balinese beef cheek curry and roast pork belly, as well as lots of sides like gado gado and sambal.

🏠 Jalan Petitenget, 100x

☎ +62 3618465950

🖱 merahputihbali.com

📘 Merah Putih Bali

📷 @merahputihbali

🕑 Mon - Sun 12pm - 3pm,
6pm - 11.30pm

Sarong

(8) *Asian Fusion Flavours*

Part of the same family of restaurants as one of my all time favourites *Mama San* (as well as *Hujan Locale* in Ubud), *Sarong* is the sophisticated older sister, with a slightly more traditional and somewhat more 'romantic' vibe. Asian fusion at its finest, *Sarong* is helmed by chef Will Meyrick who travels far and wide for research and ingredients sourcing trips. I love the blend of Asian flavours, with creative dishes such as Indian-Chinese-style dumplings with pork and mango pickle, Sri Lankan apple eggplant curry, Southern Thai-style grilled beef cheek or Tandoori ajwani seafood tikka with prawn, fish and squid. As it is often booked up, make sure to call in advance to bag a table at this tasty joint – note that it's only open for dinner.

🏠 Jalan Petitenget, 19X

📞 +62 81236343386

🖱 sarongbali.com

✉ info@sarongbali.com

📷 @sarongrestaurant

🕐 Mon - Sun 6.30pm – 12am

Barbacoa

(9) *Smokey South American Grill*

When you walk into this rustic warehouse, the first thing you'll notice is the huge open fire stacked with logs, slowly barbecuing a whole pig. You can safely say that this isn't the best place for vegetarians. Taking inspiration for its food from South America, *Barbacoa* brings the asado-style atmosphere of an Argentinian social gathering to Bali. The tapas type dishes encourage you to try a big portion of their menu, from Cuban pulled pork sliders, Peruvian snapper ceviche to the more meaty charcoal-grilled beef rib eye. If you come for lunch you can sit out on the terrace overlooking the lovely rice paddy fields. For dinner, get stuck into their cocktail menu. I recommend the 'Silent Assassin' with chilli vodka, raspberry and coriander root.

🏠 Jalan Petitenget, 14

☎ +62 81239999825

⬉ barbacoabali.com

✉ info@barbacoabali.com

f Barbacoa

⚬ @barbacoabali

⊘ Mon - Sun 12pm - 12am

Sardine

⑩ *Serene Seafood Setting*

Get a feel for the 'old Bali' whist dining next to rice paddy fields in the breezy bamboo structures at *Sardine*. Flocks of ducks run around, dipping in and out of the water while the farmers tend to the rice. Come evening, the fields are softly lit by lights under decorative umbrellas. As the name suggests, *Sardine* focuses mainly on seafood, sourcing their catch from the nearby fishing village of Jimbaran. The menu changes daily due to what's best at the market. You'll be tucking into delightful dishes such as yellowfin tuna carpaccio, pan seared wild snapper and barramundi in banana leaf. This is a lovely place to come for dinner, but you'll need to call in advance to make a reservation, as *Sardine* is a popular spot. Alternatively, pop in for lunch or come for a pre-dinner cocktail when reservations aren't required.

🏠 Jalan Petitenget, 21

📞 +62 8113978333

🢔 sardinebali.com

✉ sardine@sardinebali.com

📘 Sardine

🕙 Mon - Sun 11.30am - 1am

Grow

11 *Sustainable & Seasonal Food*

One of my top spots for a weekend lunch in Singapore is *Open Farm Community*, so I was excited to hear that the same chef, Ryan Clift, had opened up his first restaurant in Bali; *Grow*. A good place for a delicious lunch, as well as dinner, *Grow* champions the values of sustainability and farm-to-table cooking, using fresh ingredients sourced from Bali and Indonesia. The modern menu is seasonal, depending on what's good at the time, such as fish from Lombok, beef from East Java, and basil and apples from Kintamani in Bali. Come during the day and have the 3-course lunch menu with dishes such as tuna ceviche, carrot and cardamom spaghettoni, and lemon and thyme panna cotta. Pop upstairs to *Grow-Up* bar for a passionfruit and strawberry mojito at sunset.

🏠 Jalan Petitenget, 8L

☎ +62 3618947908

↖ growbali.com

✉ info@growbali.com

📘 Grow

📷 @grow.bali

◷ Mon – Sun 7am – 12am

La Favela

12 *Design Lovers' Drinking Den*

A blink-and-you'll-miss-it entrance hides the enchanting Brazilian-inspired bar and restaurant *La Favela*. Walk under leafy vines down an alleyway and into an overgrown cobbled courtyard with tables dotted beneath shady trees. Step beyond the peeling painted doors and you are transported to the living quarters of a family from Rio. Floral laminated cloths cover the dining tables surrounded by mismatched chairs. Kitsch collectibles, faux flowers and framed Virgin Mary pictures decorate the rooms, with 1950's era television sets and pastel coloured cabinets making you feel as if you're hanging out in someone's home. The owners declare that '*Favela*' is a community and welcome people from all walks of life. The food they serve is Mediterranean meets Latin America, while the cocktail menu offers a mix of classics as well as their signature drinks, such as 'Favela Breeze' with peach liqueur and dragon fruit.

🏠 Jalan Laksmana, 177X

☎ +62 361730010

↖ lafavela.com

✉ balilafavela@gmail.com

📘 La Favela Bali

📷 lafavelabali_

🕐 Mon - Sun 5pm - 3am

Motel Mexicola

13 *Kitsch Cocktail Charmer*

Step inside the crazy 1960's world of Latino-loving *Motel Mexicola* and, no, this isn't some seedy Miami-style hotel. Bold, bright and beautiful, this restaurant and bar has endless nooks and corners decorated with hand-painted murals, pots of cactuses and framed photos of tropical-styled ladies, like Carmen Miranda. This place is great for a party, so bring along a group of pals and get stuck into their tequila-drenched cocktails and comfort food snacks, such as pork empanadas, chorizo quesadillas and fish tacos. The atmosphere here is friendly and fun, with loud music bouncing off the walls and margaritas flowing from the bar. Show off your moves on the dance floor after a frozen daiquiri or two.

🏠 Jalan Kayu Jati, 9X

☎ +62 361736688

🡵 motelmexicolabali.com

f Motel Mexicola

⊙ @motelmexicola

⊘ Mon - Sun 11am - 1am

Potato Head Beach Club

14 *Party in a Pool*

A trip to Bali isn't complete without a good few hours spent propping up the swim-up bar at *Potato Head*. Somewhat of an iconic landmark in Seminyak, *Potato Head* is a huge open air space known best for its long, turquoise infinity pool set beside a stretch of sandy beach. This is a daytime drinking kind of place. The cocktails are masterminded by legendary mixologist Dre Masso, taking inspiration from the venue's tropical location to come up with creations using homemade ingredients like lemongrass gin, vanilla sugar and strawberry foam. If you're planning to be here for a while, you'll want to grab a daybed so arrive early to ensure you get a spot. Alternatively, you can sit on a submerged bar stool and float around in the pool with a glass of rosé in hand. Classy!

🏠 Jalan Petitenget, 51B

☎ +62 3614737979

🏹 ptthead.com

✉ phbc.reservation@pttfamily.com

f Potato Head Beach Club Bali

◉ @pttheadbali

⊘ Mon - Sun 10am - 2am

Kim Soo

15 *Indonesian-inspired Homewares*

If there was ever a shop to inspire you to give your home a total overhaul, it's *Kim Soo*. What I love about shopping for homeware in Bali is that the pieces are so interesting and unique, and luckily relatively affordable. Taking artefacts and designs from all over the Indonesian archipelago, pick up anything and everything from traditional Borneo tobacco baskets, Papua-inspired necklaces on stands and Javanese-style wooden Dingklik benches to more contemporary items such as crochet cushions, shells with copper details, and marble serving platters. Reflecting the old combined with the new concept is the lovely space that the store is housed in – an old Dutch building with gorgeous arches and open-air spaces. There's also a fab cafe on site with fresh and tasty cakes and good coffee.

🏠 Jalan Kayu Aya, 21

☎ +62 82247130122

↖ kimsoohome.com

✉ bali@kimsoohome.com

📘 Kim Soo

📷 @kimsoohome

🕐 Mon – Sun 9am – 10pm

The Bali Tailor

16 *Made-to-measure Leather*

If, like me, you've been on a never-ending quest for the perfect leather jacket that will last you a lifetime, then I've found just the place for you. Located on Jalan Beraban, a quiet back road in Seminyak, *The Bali Tailor* has the most stylish showroom filled with buttery leather jackets, soft-suede dresses, beautiful belts and the sassiest shoes. After a design consultation with the talented local tailors, allow five working days for them to create your own unique one-off piece. You can choose your own leather, hardware and style using example designs they have, or alternatively you can show them a photo of your dream jacket to recreate. They quoted around 3 million Rp ($210) for a leather jacket and 1.5 million Rp ($105) for a pair of leather shoes or boots, which I think is fair for a bespoke creation. Don't miss their homeware store *The Tailored Home* across the road, where you can order customised leather and wood chairs as well as cool pieces off-the-peg.

🏠 Jalan Beraban, 67

📍 thebalitailor.com

✉️ hello@thebalitailor.com

📘 The Bali Tailor

📷 @thebalitailor

🕐 Mon – Sat 9am – 6pm
Sun 10am – 4pm

Magali Pascal

17 *Chic Parisian Pieces*

If you're a fan of the elegant stores that line the streets of Paris, then you'll love this French designer's space in Seminyak. One of the higher-end brands in the neighbourhood, *Magali Pascal* (also the name of the designer) stocks stylish and luxurious clothes that are as easy to wear in the city as on the island. Her runway-worthy pieces are designed for special events, such as the couture-style dresses made using sheer lace fabrics and silk chiffon panelling. There are also more everyday outfits like blue and white-striped playsuits that would look fitting while walking along the beaches of Biarritz. Pascal has got the Paris-meets-Bali look down to a T, with vintage inspired light cotton smock dresses and floaty gypsy maxi skirts. Don't miss a look into this bohemian boutique.

⌂ Jalan Laksmana, 177X

☎ +62 361736147

🔾 magalipascal.com

🔲 Magali Pascal

🔲 @magalipascal

🕑 Mon - Sun 9am - 9.30pm

Biasa

(18) *Italian-inspired Resort wear*

🏠 Jalan Raya Seminyak, 36

☎ +62 361 730699

🏹 biasagroup.com

📘 BiasaOfficial

📷 @biasaofficial

⏲ Mon – Sun 9am – 9pm

The beautiful *Biasa* is one of those shops that *looks* expensive (which is probably what prevented me from going in for so long), without actually being it, luckily. My assumption must be down to the fact that the Italian designer and founder, Susanna Perini, was born into a family of couturiers, and this style, elegance and level of quality has seeped into this tropical-inspired Bali brand. I'm a little bit in love with the floaty apricot-orange jumpsuit that I picked up there, and beyond obsessed with the strappy soft-leather sandals that I found. The styles, shapes and textures of the fabrics have a distinctly Italian feel, while at the same time catering to the hot Balinese climate. Come here for show-stopping structured dresses, loose-linen beach wrap-arounds, sophisticated striped shirts, and light tailored suits. They also do really lovely pieces for men. *Biasa* have a few stores in Seminyak as well as branches in Ubud and Jakarta.

Uma & Leopold

19 *Brazil Meets Bali*

Designer Lara Braga moved from her native Rio de Janeiro to live the island life in Bali, where she now works with local craftsmen to produce feminine but edgy summery clothes. Items can take a month to create, using techniques such as Indonesian Karawang embroidery, hand beading and leather weaving. She stocks special pieces to fill up your wardrobe, from silk maxi dresses with lace trimmings, sophisticated shirt dresses to soft structured leather jackets. As well as clothes, *Uma & Leopold* sell stylish shoes, like their platform leather sandals and tanned gladiators. Channel your inner glamazon with their sleek and chic pieces.

⌂ Jalan Oberoi, 77X

☎ + 62 361737697

➤ umaandleopold.com

🄵 uma and leopold

🄾 @umaandleopold

⊘ Mon - Sun 10am - 8pm

Lulu Yasmine

20 *Bohemian Handmade Attire*

This Bali-born brand encompasses the nomadic lifestyle — clothes made for women who hop on adventures around the globe. The travel theme comes from Luiza Chang, a Chinese-Brazilian who grew up in Brazil before living in Europe and then basing herself in Asia. This mix of cultures is reflected in the designs, which can be described as beach-ready resort wear with a nod to European elegance. Find long silk evening dresses and cream shorts with colourful beaded pockets, alongside French pearly silk lingerie. Some of the prices might be slightly higher than in other stores, but what you're paying for are special one-off pieces for your wardrobe that have been handcrafted on the island.

🏠 Jalan Laksmana, 100X

☎ +62 361736763

➤ luluyasmine.com

📘 Lulu Yasmine

📷 @luluyasmine

🕐 Mon - Sun 9am - 9pm

Escalier + Canaan

21 *Beachside Lifestyle Stores*

Catering to the international jet-set crowd that flows through the doors of *Potato Head Beach Club*, *Escalier* is a carefully curated store that selects fresh and fun brands from across the globe. With a focus on resort wear, the shop sells swimwear from favourites like Kiini, Fella and Mara Hoffman alongside playful slogan sunglasses from Wildfox. Across the road is the artisan-style store *Canaan*. This charming shop sources handmade goods from Indonesia as well as overseas. Find blue-dyed narrow textiles from West Timor used as a shoulder cloth for ceremonies, or intricate ikat fabrics, as well as lovely ceramic collections and *Canaan's* own candles.

🏠 Jalan Petitenget, 51B
(at Potato Head Beach Club)

↖ escalier-store.com,
canaanbali.com

📷 @escalierstore, @canaan_bali

🕐 Mon - Sun 11am - 11pm

Seminyak Flea Market

22 *Bali's Bargains*

I used to dismiss this market, thinking that it was simply a bunch of stalls selling tacky tourist souvenirs and t-shirts with beer brand logos. Okay, so it might have a bit of that as well, but if you look past this you will find a treasure trove of bargains. My first stop is the stand that sells brightly-coloured embroidered clutch bags and cushions. You should aim to spend around $10 and $15 respectively on these, but you'll need to haggle here (as well as throughout the market). Stock up on crochet bikinis, shorts, throws and bags that are handmade locally on the island; these should cost you around $10 per piece. Don't miss the lovely stand selling silk kaftans and kimonos – perfect pieces for wafting around the beach bars in.

🏠 Jalan Kayu Aya, near the entrance to *The Oberoi* hotel

🕐 Mon - Sun 9am - 9pm

Jalan Raya Kerobokan

 Homeware and Textile Treasures

Lucy's Batik

If you're after homeware bargains, then get off the main streets of Seminyak with their fancy styled stores and onto the scruffier looking Jalan Raya Kerobokan. Pop into *Dalle Art* where for a couple of Indonesian notes you can pick up a white feather tribal necklace, mermaid-like shell jewellery boxes and mother of pearl trays. Nearby, *Selected Living* sells contemporary wooden furniture and home accessories as well as terracotta pots and weaved baskets. There's also a fun shop called *Magic Fish*, which specialises in recycled wood, selling carved doors and colourful curiosities. For fabrics, I like *Lucy's Batik*, down the road on Jalan Raya Basangkasa, selling authentic ikat hand-woven in Bali and beautiful brightly coloured batik from Java.

 Lucy's Batik (textiles)
Jalan Raya Basangkasa, 88

 lucysbatik.com

 Mon - Sun 9.30am - 9pm

Dalle Art

Magic Fish

Selected Living

🏠 Dalle Art (handicrafts)
Jalan Raya Kerobokan, 80

🏠 Selected Living (home
accessories and furniture)
Jalan Raya Kerobokan, 115

🏠 Magic Fish (recycled wood)
Jalan Raya Kerobokan, 120

Bodyworks

 Blissful Urban Oasis

After pounding the pavements going from shop to shop in Seminyak, you're going to need a bit of pampering. Housed in a light and airy Moroccan riad-style building, *Bodyworks* is the place to go for a classic day spa experience that Bali is so well known for. Sit outside in the peaceful, plant-filled orange courtyard and be treated to a relaxing foot massage or pedicure. They're renowned for their traditional Indonesian healing techniques, from the signature two-hour exfoliation massage, known locally as Mandi Lulur, to hot stone massages using ancient forms of healing. The spa is great value for money, so you can easily spend all afternoon here undergoing treatment after treatment. The vibe of the spa is welcoming to both males and females – so girls, bring along your other halves.

🏠 Jalan Kayu Jati, 2

☎ +62 361733317

🖱 bodyworksbali.com

f Bodyworks Spa Bali

📷 @bodyworksbali

🕐 Mon - Sun 9am - 10pm

Rob Peetoom

25 *Hair Spa with a View*

Dutch hair guru Rob Peetoom hopped over from the Netherlands to open a stylish hair spa in Seminyak. The Asian-inspired buildings have a serene and spiritual energy, whilst feeling über glam. For those precious about their locks, look no further as stylists are trained to exact European standards, so you can get a half-head of highlights or a cut and blow dry with confidence. Offering more than just hair care, for a truly spoiling experience, book yourself in for a pedicure overlooking the tranquil rice paddies. *Rob Peetoom* feels really posh, but luckily the prices are purse friendly so you can have a luxurious experience without the guilt. I'd definitely recommend this place if you want a quiet afternoon of 'me time' in peaceful and plush surroundings.

⌂ Jalan Petitenget, 16

☎ +62 361738363

➹ robpeetoom.nl

✉ bali@robpeetoom.nl

⊙ @robpeetoombali

⊙ Mon – Tues 12pm – 8pm
Wed – Sun 10am – 8pm

Katamama

26 *Hip 'n' Happening Hotel*

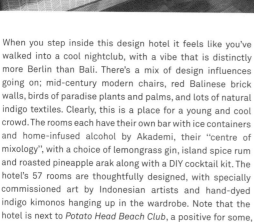

When you step inside this design hotel it feels like you've walked into a cool nightclub, with a vibe that is distinctly more Berlin than Bali. There's a mix of design influences going on; mid-century modern chairs, red Balinese brick walls, birds of paradise plants and palms, and lots of natural indigo textiles. Clearly, this is a place for a young and cool crowd. The rooms each have their own bar with ice containers and home-infused alcohol by Akademi, their "centre of mixology", with a choice of lemongrass gin, island spice rum and roasted pineapple arak along with a DIY cocktail kit. The hotel's 57 rooms are thoughtfully designed, with specially commissioned art by Indonesian artists and hand-dyed indigo kimonos hanging up in the wardrobe. Note that the hotel is next to *Potato Head Beach Club*, a positive for some, but you also have the music playing when you're by the pool. Do try the restaurant *Kaum*, which is in the beach club next door, for delicious Indonesian cuisine.

🏠 Jalan Petitenget, 51B
(at Potato Head Beach Club)

🔗 katamama.com

✉ katamama@pttfamily.com

f Katamama

○ @katamama_hotel

$ From $250

Brown Feather

 Boutique B&B

I fondly remember arriving at *Brown Feather* after a jaunt to the Gili Islands (where I stayed at a scruffy backpacker's hostel) and feeling like I'd arrived in heaven. It was also the same price as said hostel, which made me even more impressed. At Rp450k per night, or about $30, *Brown Feather* is amazing value for money. It's a little boutique B&B slightly out of town on Batu Belig, but they give you free use of electric bicycles to whizz into Seminyak in no time. The cast iron beds are beyond comfortable, and I love the vintage Singer sewing machine basins and the all over homely design. If you're in Seminyak for a night or two and want something cheap and cheerful then *Brown Feather* is your place.

🏠 Jalan Batu Belig, 100

☎ +62 3614732165

↖ brownfeather.com

✉ booking@brownfeather.com

📷 @brownfeatherhotel

💲 From $30

The Island Houses

28 *Stunning & Spacious Villas*

🏠 Jalan Sari Dewi

↖ theislandhouses.com

✉ bookings@theislandhouses.com

⭘ @theislandhouses

$ From $230

I was never that keen on staying in the centre of Seminyak, until I discovered the paradise that is *The Island Houses*. These impeccably designed villas are each so spacious, you'd never believe you're in the middle of town. Quiet and calm, the only sound to be heard is of the birds tweeting and the breeze rushing through the palms. For design addicts, the interiors are jaw-dropping. The style is warm and cosy; imagine Morocco-meets-Bali with thick hand-woven rugs, tall ceilings with beautiful beams, colourful velvet cushions and luxurious French linen on all the beds. Uniquely designed and styled, the six villas have one to three bedrooms. For couples, there's the one-bedroom Pandan House, and for groups and families, I love Desu House. Africa House has rustic circular pods for bedrooms and the most gorgeous pool. If you're planning to stay in Seminyak — stay here!

Canggu

Hip and Happening 'Hood

Since the streets of Seminyak have become busier, travellers in the know have decamped to Canggu, the trendy and low-key neighbourhood next door. There's a lovely sense of community here. Being the area of choice for many of the island's expats, the vibe is more akin to a place that people live, rather than a tourist destination. After spending a few days in Canggu, it's easy to feel at home.

Mornings in Canggu start at the crack of dawn, when half the 'hood hop on their bikes down to Batu Bolong or Echo's to tackle the swell. Salty-skinned surfers and golden-limbed honeys then gather over cups of caffeine at one of Canggu's hip coffee hangouts.

While Seminyak is stylish and sophisticated, Canggu is cool and casual. The crowd is young and fun, and there's an atmosphere of creativity and collaboration on every corner. Designers, photographers and artists thrive on the environment of experimentation and opportunity.

Days are spent enjoying lazy lunches by the beach or snacking at healthy organic cafes. Evenings get lively, when cool kids gather to watch guitar-wielding bands.

Book yourself into a breezy open-air villa near the beach with a private pool. Thankfully they're affordable as well as plentiful, so it's easy to find a place to crash even if it's a last minute trip. Seminyak is just a short drive down the shore for more fancy food and bustling bars.

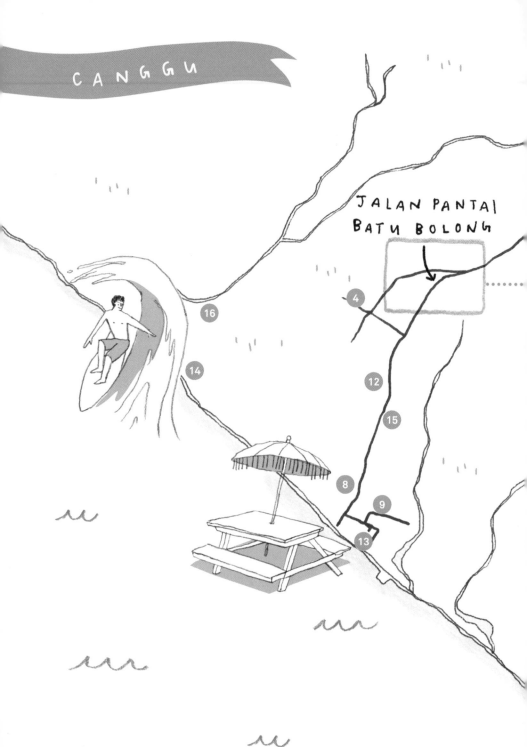

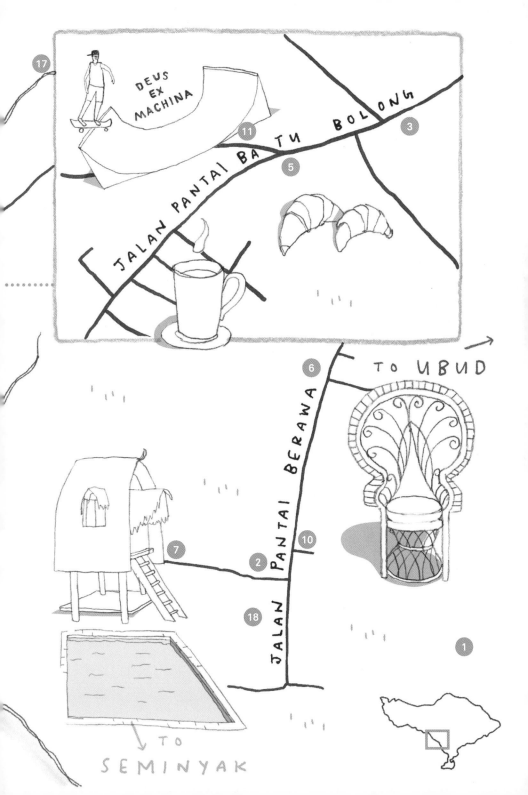

Remix

1 *Small & Cosy Cafe*

My lovely friend and Canggu local showed me this special spot, *Remix*, and I found myself returning to this cafe day after day. It's easy to drive past and miss this little hole-in-the-wall cafe, a small space with only a few chairs and tables for customers, nestled in the Umalas neighbourhood on the edge of Canggu. *Remix* is generally known for its cold press juices, which they make in their kitchen using local, organic produce. I personally fell more for their delicious dirty chai coffee and the most dreamy cheese omelette with sautéed veg on the side. For lunch they have healthy choices like zucchini soba chow mein and Asian vermicelli salad with tempeh and cucumber. I also like how this place is quiet and low-key, so you can start your day off with a relaxing breakfast without the crowds found at other cafes in the area!

🏠 Jalan Umalas II, 16A

📞 +62 361 8974005

🖱 remixjuicebali.com

📘 Remix Juice Bali

📷 @remixjuicebali

🕐 Mon – Sat 7am – 4pm
Closed Sun

Peloton Supershop

2 *Plant-based Brekkie*

🏠 Jalan Raya Pantai Berawa, 46

☎ +62 81337619335

↖ pelotonsupershop.com

📷 @pelotonsupershop

🕐 Mon – Sun 7.30am – 10pm

After a morning yoga session at the wonderful *Desa Seni*, make your way to the hip plant-based cafe *Peloton Supershop* just across the road on Berawa. A great spot for breakfast, this vegan cafe serves mostly organic and local produce. I always get the 'breakaway burrito,' a coriander-infused tortilla with scrambled tofu, Mexican beans and cashew sour cream. For the prettiest meal, get a side to share of 'moonshine morning'; a super fruity bowl with dragon fruit, banana, cacao and spirulina topped with fruit, seeds and flower petals. Along with organic coffee, they use fresh nut milks that are made every morning; I get a flat white with coconut milk. They also do their bit to be eco by using special corn straws instead of plastic, and they also donate their used oils to the *Green School* to fuel their bio bus.

Cafe Vida

3 *Healthy Canggu Cafe*

Another great tip from a Canggu local is the lovely *Cafe Vida*. Friends of mine can't get enough of it and go most days, and after trying this cool cafe I can see why. Located within a traditional Balinese compound, there's a lovely relaxing courtyard garden to sit in. For those on a health kick, they've got immunity detox booster shots, such as turmeric, ginger and black pepper, chili tea vinegar and raw honey and activated charcoal with aloe vera. To start the day, I love the 'vitality green breakfast bowl' with organic steamed kale and asparagus, quinoa and poached eggs with the tastiest sauces of beetroot hummus and pesto (no ketchup here!). They've also got a great selection of raw and gluten free cakes. I adore the cinnamon swirl made with banana flour, and the raw and vegan lemon and raspberry cheesecake is a must try.

🏠 Jalan Pantai Batu Bolong, 38A

☎ +62 81339886864

📘 Cafe Vida

📷 @cafe_vida_bali

🕐 Mon – Sun 7am – 10.30pm

The Shady Shack

4 *Delicious Vegetarian Dishes*

In this Balinese neighbourhood, it's all about the breakfasts. Swing by *The Shady Shack* for one of the tastiest brekkies around. Founded by a free-spirited Aussie chick called Gypsy, (who also runs the popular *Betelnut* across the road), this white-washed wooden cafe serves up vegetarian and vegan dishes. I love the 'chickbeans'; 64 degree onsen eggs with Spanish braised chickpeas and mashed avo, whilst slurping on the bright purple 'bliss berry' smoothie with blueberry, coconut yoghurt and bee pollen. There's a laid back vibe to the cafe, and I love the layout, with wooden tables placed underneath leafy palm trees and gorgeous décor, like the peacock chairs and benches with cosy cushions on the veranda.

Jalan Tanah Barak, 53

+62 81916395087

@theshadyshack

Mon – Sun 7.30am – 10.30pm

Monsieur Spoon

5 *Flavoursome French Bakery*

Masterminded by a Parisian pastry chef, *Monsieur Spoon* is a small French bakery filling that croissant-shaped hole in the Canggu breakfast scene. Pop in for a classic combo of coffee, flaky croissants and jam, fill up on avocado and eggs or tuck into a traditional Croque-Madame. The founders are passionate about using top quality ingredients in their food, whether it's an almond chocolatine or a pistachio macaroon. Be careful though, a regular routine of starting your day at *Monsieur Spoon* can soon become an addiction. I have a friend who banned himself from here to avoid an expanding waistline. I probably shouldn't tell you that the cafe also delivers. It's a dangerous place for anyone working on his or her beach body.

🏠 Jalan Pantai Batu Bolong, 55

☎ +62 87862808859

➤ monsieurspoon.com

f Monsieur Spoon

◎ @monsieurspoon

◷ Mon - Sun 6.30am - 9pm

Campur Asia

6 *Delicious Japanese Deli*

With its blink-and-you'll-miss-it location just up the road from *Bungalow Living* on Berawa, *Campur Asia* is a small and casual deli frequented by foodies in the know. This low-key dining spot is rooted in Japanese and Asian home cooking. The focus is on fresh and flavoursome food, with dishes like Thai green curry noodle soup, ahi poke bowl with raw tuna, and Vietnamese spring rolls on the menu. For an extra boost, you can slurp wheatgrass shots knocked back with homemade lemon ice tea or a mango berry frappé. The design is cosy and slightly kitsch, with mismatched outdoor seating and a newer, cooler indoor area. They also have a display of colourful vintage Asian crockery on sale for you to take home with you.

 Jalan Pantai Berawa, 17

 +62 3618868787

campurasia.com

Mon – Sat 11am – 7pm

Ulekan

(7) *Casual Contemporary Indonesian*

A wonderful, casual Indonesian restaurant, *Ulekan* was created by the people behind my fave Seminyak spot *Watercress*, and is a top choice for dinner in Canggu. The Javanese word ulekan translates to 'pestle', reflecting the spices and flavours of Indonesia that go into each dish. It's best to come with a big group, as lots of the dishes are for sharing. I particularly liked the chicken curry, 'kare ayam', with coconut, turmeric, kaffir lime and lemongrass, and the 'pepes ikan', which is the steamed fish in banana leaf with Balinese spices. The vegetable starters like gado gado and tahu tek are a dream too. For those who like spice make sure you order a selection of the sambal, each variety reflecting the region that it comes from. I'm a little bit obsessed the iced teas that they do here – I could drink gallons of the lemongrass, ginger and pandan leaf tea. They're also open for lunch and do a delicious nasi campur with a variety of bites; beef rendang, organic chicken, sweet corn fritters and crunchy tempeh.

🏠 Jalan Tegal Sari, 34
Pantai Berawa

☎ +62 813 39211466

🔦 ulekanbali.com

✉ hello@ulekanbali.com

📘 Ulekan Bali

📷 @ulekanbali

🕐 Mon – Sun 11am – 10pm

Ji

8 *Cultural Dining Spot*

🏠 Jalan Pantai Batu Bolong

☎ +62 3614731701

🏹 jiatbalesutra.com

✉ ji@tuguhotels.com

📘 Ji Restaurant Bali

📷 @jirestaurantbali

🕐 Mon – Sun 12pm – 12am

I first fell in love with the Tugu hotels while in Lombok, staying at their place in the north of the island with some girlfriends. There we learnt about the interesting story of the founder, Anhar Setjadibrata, who is one of the biggest collectors of Indonesian fine art and cultural antiquities in Indonesia, and who started these museum-like hotels to house and showcase his unique collection. The *Hotel Tugu* in Canggu is home to the wonderful *Ji*; a restaurant and bar, located on the shore at Batu Bolong Beach. Japanese in influence, they serve up tasty dishes such as yellowfin tuna tataki, scallop and snapper ceviche, and snacks like nigiri sushi and maki rolls. If you're looking for really good sunset cocktails, this is the place. Head up the stairs to *Ji terrace by the sea*, and order a refreshing Tugu gin and tea, with naga tea infused Tanqueray. Come for sunset for the best view of the beach and surfers in action.

Old Man's

(9) *Happening Beach Hangout*

After a couple of days spent in Canggu, you'll feel yourself naturally gravitating back to *Old Man's* time and time again. This place is sort of everything for everyone. Early bird surfers can roll in here straight out of the water, rinse under the outdoor showers and then fill up on bacon and egg rolls or banana porridge. If you're with a group of friends, come here for a lazy lunch and graze on good old burgers and chips washed down with a couple of glasses of wine. The food is simple pub grub, but the prices are good and it's an easy-going, relaxed environment. Come evening, perch under a palm tree on one of their wooden benches for a sunset cocktail or two. Do look out for the market, held on the last Saturday of the month. You'll find one-off vintage clothes and statement jewellery as well as freshly-baked cakes.

🏠 Jalan Pantai Batu Bolong (by the beach)

☎ +62 3618469158

📘 Old Man's

📷 @oldmansbali

🕐 Mon - Sun 7am - 1am

Bungalow Living

10 *Lovely Lifestyle Store*

🏠 Jalan Pantai Berawa, 35A

☎ +62 3618446567

🗦 bungalowlivingbali.com

📘 Bungalow Living Bali

📷 @bungalowlivingcafe

🕗 Mon - Sun 8am - 6pm

Bungalow Living is a heavenly homeware store that cleverly doubles up as a charming cafe. The space is styled like you're in the home of someone really fabulous, and of course the best bit is you can buy all the lovely things that you see on the shelves. Stock up on pom pom fringed embroidered cushions, Indian cotton bed linen, handmade banana leaf storage baskets and colourful quilts. There are cosy corners in the cafe where you can sit down for a coffee or dragon fruit smoothie while deciding on how much you can take home in your suitcase. Opposite the cafe is the *Bungalow gallery*, where you can find bigger pieces such as white peacock chairs, decorative birdcages and wall art. *Bungalow Living* is a great shop to find gifts for friends or to kit out your home.

Deus Ex Machina

11 *Bikes, Boards, Brunch and Bands*

🏠 Jalan Pantai Batu Mejan, 8

☎ +62 811388315

↖ deuscustoms.com

📘 Deus Bali

📷 @deustemple

◔ 7am - 12am

Deus (pronounced 'day-us') is a creative den for those that like to get high on caffeine and gasoline. The main shop is filled with beefy motorbikes, custom shaped boards and racks of graphic printed t-shirts (for those of us not cool enough for the main items on sale). Come here to browse the bikes, and stay for brunch and coffee in the so-called 'Temple of Enthusiasm'. If you like to get inked, make sure you're around for their 'Tacos 'n' Tatt Tuesdays', when you can get tequilas and complimentary tattoos on tap. Sunday nights are where it's at, when the whole of Canggu descends on *Deus* to watch raucous live bands and drink beer and mojitos.

Spring Spa

12 *Stylish & Sophisticated Spa*

The sister to the Seminyak outpost, this chic and airy spa on Batu Bolong is the place to go for sophisticated treatments in a calm and clean environment. You'll immediately feel relaxed when you walk into the white-walled Japanese-style open-air spa with treatment rooms dotted around a fresh water pond. For those who have spent the morning in the surf at Old Man's, why not treat yourself to a Balinese massage, or if you've been basking in the sun for too long, have a 'cool as a cucumber' face mask to remove the heat from sun-blasted skin. They do everything else from pedicures and manicures to facials and body scrubs. If your hair is feeling a bit flat, they have a 'get up and glow' package, with blow dry, hair treatment and nail polish – what a treat! While more fancy than some other spas, *Spring* manages to maintain good-value pricing and feels very professional.

🏠 Jalan Pantai Batu Bolong, 83c

☎ +62 853 3844 7500

🡒 springspa.com

✉ canggu@springspa.com

📷 @spring_spa

🕑 Mon – Sun 9am – 9pm

Batu Bolong Beach

13 *Black Sand Beach*

A world away from the white coloured beaches of The Bukit, Canggu has the more typical Balinese volcanic black sand lining its shores. Batu Bolong Beach is best known amongst the surfers that paddle in from early morning 'til dusk. It's also a spot for the local surf camps that reside in Canggu – there are plenty around if you want to step up your surf game over a week or so. There are stacks of boards for hire by the beach and surf instructors on hand for lessons too. With the current being so strong it isn't advised for swimmers, so it's perhaps best to paddle, lounge around on the beach or go for a barefoot stroll. Pop into *Old Man's* just behind the beach for a bite to eat and shade from the midday sun.

🏠 Jalan Pantai Batu Bolong

Echo Beach

 Quiet Surfers' Spot

Known locally as Pantai Batu Mejan, Echo Beach is similar to its neighbouring beach, Batu Bolong, with its black volcanic sand and surf-worthy waves. A scattering of simple warungs and a couple of restaurants line the shore, serving up local Indonesian food and seafood BBQs come evening. Big, comfy beanbags, sun loungers and umbrellas are dotted on the sand so you can chill and watch the surfers at play. Although the beach isn't your idyllic, tropical postcard perfection, it's quiet and uncrowded, and there's something quite unique about the black sand under your feet. A popular place for surfers, the waves can be quite rough for swimmers, although it's nice for a shallow paddle. 'Echo's', as it's called, is a lovely place to come for a couple of beers come sunset.

 Jalan Pantai Batu Mejan

The Slow

15 *Trendy Tropical Hideaway*

The accommodation choices in Canggu tend to be predominantly villas, but if you want a boutique hotel experience, *The Slow* is the hip and trendy pick. The small 12-room hotel is in a great location on Batu Bolong, so you can easily walk everywhere from here whether that's to the surf at Old Man's or the cafes in central Canggu. There's a cool Californian vibe to the hotel (they stream music from LA's Reverberation Radio), and the rooms balance concrete wall brutalism with a tropical feel created by palm trees in the corners. The owners are into their art too, with a special rotation of art pieces decorating all the walls. Even if you're not staying here, you can enjoy their all-day dining. They do fabulous small tapas dishes infusing cuisines from the chef's travels through Europe, South America and Asia. The cocktails here are pretty tasty, using specialty batch spirits and tonics.

⌂ Jalan Pantai Batu Bolong, 97

☎ +62 3612099000

↖ theslow.id

✉ Info@theslow.id

⊙ @the.slow

$ From $180

Villa Phoenix

16 *Beautiful Boho Surf Pad*

This bohemian hideaway is positioned a stone's throw away from Echo Beach – close enough to hear the waves crashing while you lounge by the pool, and if you hop up to the second floor balcony you're in a good position to do a surf check. A two-bedroom villa that can be rented by the room, what strikes you is the level of design and detail that has gone into making this place a home. The villa is filled with art found locally in Bali as well as artefacts picked up from around the world. The whole space is designed for outdoor living, from the open-air kitchen and living room, to the lush green plants dotted in every corner.

🏠 Echo Beach

↖ airbnb.com/rooms/899419

$ From $94

Kalapa Resort

17 *Affordable Hidden Hotel*

🏠 Jalan Raya Uma Buluh, 14

☎ +62 3618445650

↖ kalapabali.com

✉ info@kalapabali.com

📷 @kalapabali

💲 From $100

If you're looking for a reasonably priced, intimate but spacious resort away from any hustle and bustle, then *Kalapa* is a good choice. With tastefully designed and furnished villas and bungalows starting from $100 a night, including breakfast and yoga, it really is great value for money. The eight-room resort is designed like a traditional Indonesian village, with Balinese daybeds with comfy cushions dotted around, and two lovely swimming pools, one looking over a lush rice field. They also provide complimentary yoga each morning in an old-style wooden joglo hut. The resort never feels crowded, and you'll often find that you have one of the pools all to yourself to enjoy. The location of *Kalapa*, slightly north of Canggu, is quite far from the beach, so take this into consideration (you have to use a bike to get around as it's too far to walk).

Desa Seni

18 *Holistic and Rustic Retreat*

If you want to find the most peaceful place to recharge and revive, pay a visit to the eco village resort of *Desa Seni*. Designed to give you a traditional Indonesian cultural experience, you can stay in an antique wooden bungalow, attend their yoga classes of which there are four a day and be healed at their Svaasthya wellness spa. The Javanese joglo and lumbung accommodation surround a refreshing salt-water pool, which you can laze around in between your yoga and meditation sessions. *Desa Seni* puts on yoga retreats, or as a non-guest you can simply drop in and attend their group yoga classes. Conveniently located, *Desa Seni* is a ten-minute drive away from both central Canggu and Seminyak.

🏠 Jalan Subak Sari, 13

☎ +62 3618446392

🖱 desaseni.com

✉ info@desaseni.com

📘 Desa Seni

📷 @desaseni

💲 Rooms from $135 incl. breakfast and yoga. Yoga for non-guests: Rp140k.

Ubud & Surroundings

Spiritual and Serene Jungle Hideaway

Ubud is best known as the spiritual centre of Bali. Located in the heart of the island, it has long attracted the arty types drawn to its rich cultural heritage. The area surrounding Ubud is gorgeously green. Think thick foliage weaving down river valleys and chirpy birds singing in the treetops in a jungle-like setting.

The people here are artists, spiritual healers, yoga teachers and chefs who live in Ubud for the lifestyle, which is all about simplicity and being close to nature.

Home to a burgeoning festival scene in literature, music, the arts and food, Ubud has become a meeting point in Asia for like-minded souls who have a shared interest in celebrating culture.

The culinary scene is constantly evolving, with top Indonesian and international chefs setting up their kitchens here with a focus on working with the local community to source farm-fresh ingredients.

Traditional Balinese craftsmen, with skills passed down through generations, hold steady. Pockets of expert wood carvers, silversmiths and mask makers can be found in the villages around Ubud. Their passion and love for their art is untainted, and for me it is one of the most special aspects of the area.

Similar to Seminyak, Ubud's popularity has meant that this once small village has developed into a proper town. I therefore suggest you stay outside central Ubud in an adjacent village – I love staying in Penestanan or in a jungle hideaway in Tegallalang.

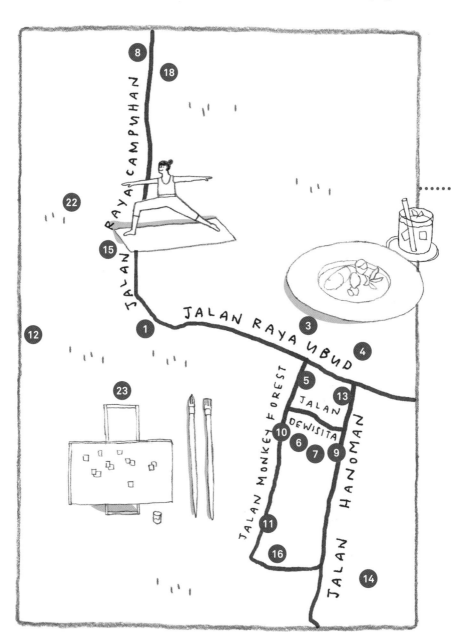

UBUD

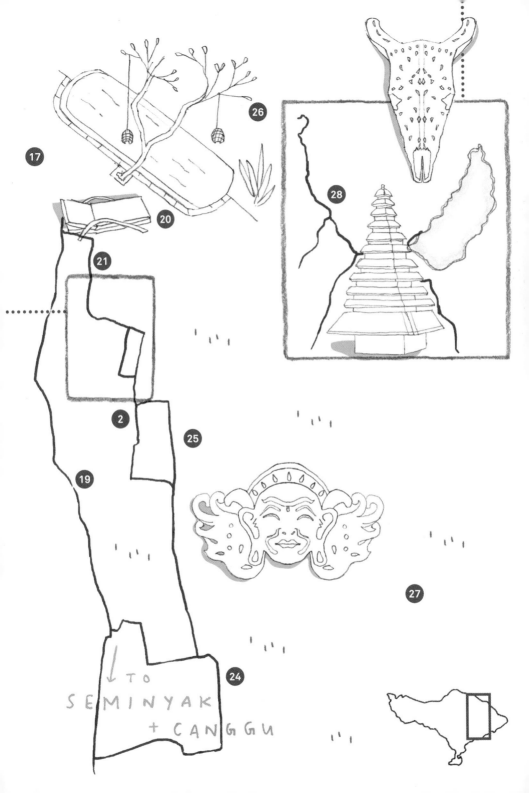

17

26

20

21

28

2

25

19

27

24

TO
SEMINYAK
+ CANGGU

Alchemy

1 *Heavenly Healthy Cafe*

If there's anywhere that can convince you to change your meat-eating ways and become a fully-fledged vegan, it's *Alchemy*. Healthy without being too hippie, *Alchemy* offers a delicious and inventive menu where your California maki sushi and nacho chips taste like the real deal. Their main event is the raw salad bar, with a serious line up including zucchini noodles, cucumber salsa and almond croutons – enough to make the most devout vegan foodie shriek with glee. Their sweets and desserts particularly impressed me, so I couldn't help but have three! Cloud 9 Cake does what is says on the tin – a light vanilla cheesecake with raspberry topping, and I'm still not sure how it's dairy free. They have a mighty long drinks menu with every fruit and veg-filled juice under the sun, which they serve with a clever eco papaya stem straw.

🏠 Jalan Penestanan Kelod, 75

📞 +62 361971981

↖ alchemybali.com

f Alchemy

🅾 @alchemybali

🕐 Mon - Sun 7am - 9pm

Wamm

(2) *Nourishing Neighbourhood Cafe*

Central Ubud can feel anything but the tranquil spot it's imagined to be, so if the traffic is getting too much, head down to the quieter neighbourhood of Nyuh Kuning, just south of the main town. The name *Wamm* arose from the conversation with the landowner, who asked '*what about my Mother?*', since his mother was running a small shop here (she still runs her activities next door). The cafe strives to provide organic, ethically and locally sourced delicious food for their customers, in a relaxed and contemporary setting. Catch up with friends for brunch and devour dishes such as 'Bali benedict' made using free-range duck eggs, or a vegan rainbow salad with raw vegetables and noodles. In the evening, the restaurant turns into *MOTHER*, with a separate menu, including innovative Asian inspired dishes with names like 'Bangkok nights' curry and 'Laos celebration', a banana blossom and green mango salad.

🏠 Jalan Nyuh Bulan, 24,
Nyuh Kuning, Mas

☎ +62 81236962663

📘 WAMM

📷 @wammbali

🕐 Wamm
Mon – Sun 7am – 5pm

Mother at Wamm
Tues – Sun 5.30pm – 12am
Closed Mon

Ibu Oka

(3) *Roast Pig Feast*

This local eating spot has built up quite the fan base – mildly helped by the fact that the famous American chef Anthony Bourdain once featured *Ibu Oka* in an episode of 'No Reservations' where he declared *'this is the best pig I've ever had!'* *Ibu Oka* serves up the traditional Indonesian dish of roasted babi guling, or suckling pig, stuffed with herbs and spices and cooked over an open flame. I personally feel that it does live up to the hype, and I never leave Ubud without a visit to this pork-filled canteen. It has recently been renovated to fit more hungry customers so it's slightly lost its rustic feel, although do ask if you can have a look out the back, where you'll see whole pigs turning on spits next to piles of logs ready to feed the fire. Come here for lunch; it's good value and extremely tasty.

⌂ Jalan Tagal Sari, 2
(behind Ubud Palace)

⊘ Mon - Sun 11am - 3pm

Hujan Locale

(4) *Modern Indonesian Cuisine*

From the people behind Seminyak's *Mama San* and *Sarong*, *Hujan Locale* is a contemporary restaurant celebrating innovative Indonesian cuisine. Its roots lie in its relationship with local farmers and the surrounding community. With many of the higher-end restaurants in Bali offering international cuisine, it's refreshing to visit a venue that stays true to its home country. Start off with the super tasty cocktails – I like 'Hujan Day' with Gin rosso, lemon, vanilla, Tabasco and cucumber. The Asian-inspired dishes are designed for sharing, so order large and get a taste of the Indonesian islands with dishes like Sulawesi salt baked baby barramundi, Sumatran barbequed pork ribs and East Java tahu tek with petis bean sprouts. A great place to come for dinner, and it's open for lunch too.

🏠 Jalan Sri Wedari, 5

☎ +62 3618493092

🏹 hujanlocale.com

✉ reservations@hujanlocale.com

📘 Hujan Locale

📷 @hujan_locale

🕐 Mon - Sun 12pm - 3pm, 5.30pm - 11pm

Locavore

5 *Fantastic Fine Dining*

🏠 Jalan Dewi Sita, 1

☎ +62 361977733

🖰 restaurantlocavore.com

✉ reservations@
    resaurantlocavore.com

f Restaurant Locavore

🕐 Tues - Sat 12pm - 2pm,
    6.30pm - 11pm,
    Mon 6.30pm - 11pm
    Closed Sun

If there is one restaurant you need to visit in Bali, it's *Locavore*. The chefs at the helm, Ray and Eelke, have created a clever concept where innovative modern dishes are produced using local ingredients. During the seven-course tasting menu you might have baby squid with squid ink and fermented leek, snails and garlic with fern tips and wild flowers, or steak tartare with mushroom and purslane leaves. The dessert is divine; I loved the white chocolate and passionfruit ganache with mangosteen sorbet and coconut jelly. They also have a Herbivore tasting menu for vegetarians. Note: due to *Locavore's* popularity you will need to book at least a few weeks in advance, which can be done on their website. Read my interview with chef Ray on p197 to learn more about their fascinating culinary story.

Nusantara

6 *Indonesian Culinary Experience*

You'll spot *Nusantara* on bustling Jalan Dewi Sita when you see the flames rising from the outdoor kitchen at the front of the restaurant, with pots bubbling and fish wrapped in banana leaf cooking on the grill. This is the new venture from the team behind *Locavore*, and it's a food experience not to be missed in Ubud. The Indonesian word nusantara translates to 'archipelago', and the focus of the restaurant is on cooking authentic and original dishes, which the team has painstakingly discovered during their research trips around Indonesia. As chef Ray says, '*if the original recipe has a lot of spice, then that's how we'll make it. We don't doctor the recipe'*. They use only the freshest seasonal Indonesian ingredients to create dishes such as smoked cakalang fish with turmeric leaves, a dish from North Sulawesi, slow-braised beef ribs with tamarind and tomatoes from East Java, and baby squid with chili and coconut milk from Central Java.

🏠 Jalan Dewi Sita

☎ +62 361977733

⚲ locavore.co.id

✉ reservations@restaurantnusantara.com

📘 Restaurant Nusantara – by Locavore

📷 @restaurantnusantara

🕐 Mon 6pm – 10pm
Tues – Sun 12pm – 2.30pm, 6pm – 10pm

Pica

7 *South American Kitchen*

Run by the most delightful duo, Cristian and Monica, *Pica* serves up South American dishes inspired by the chef's home country of Chile. Housed in a small and unassuming open-air structure on the main Dewi Sita strip, the experience at *Pica* is casual and personal. Choose from a carefully curated menu of 'ceviche nikkeo', lime marinated mahi-mahi, red onion and coriander, 'causa del mar', octopus, prawns and mahi escabeche on Peruvian cold potato cake or 'cerdo con manzana', confit pork belly and roasted sweet potatoes. The wine list here is super, stocking new world wines from South America as well as Australia and New Zealand. Save space for their dessert; I loved the 'leche asada', Chilean crème caramel.

🏠 Jalan Dewi Sita

☎ +62 361971660

🏹 picakitchen.co

✉ welcome@picakitchen.co

📘 PICA South American Kitchen

🕐 Tues - Sun 6pm - 10pm
Closed Mon

Room 4 Dessert

8 *Candy-Coated Creations*

🏠 Jalan Raya Sanggingan

📞 +62 81236662806

➤ room4dessert.asia

✉ room4dessertubud@gmail.com

📘 Room4Dessert Ubud

📷 @room4dessert_wg

⏲ Mon - Fri 5pm - 11pm,
Sat - Sun 2pm - 11pm

Calling all sweet-toothed travellers, don't miss out on an evening of culinary entertainment at the marvelous sugar-infused restaurant *Room 4 Dessert*. Will Goldfarb is the charismatic chef behind this divine joint. Originally from New York, his restaurant of the same name was the IT place in town, with celebrities like director Wes Anderson his regulars. Lured by the Ubud lifestyle, he set up camp in this unique spot where he treats customers to a tasting menu of nine carefully crafted sweet snacks paired with a selection of fine wines. Dessert dishes include Wu-Tang Clan inspired 'Ghostface Keller' with Reblochon, 'Bintang' focaccia, cocoa nibs and roasted papaya and 'taro card' with jackfruit, caramelized coconut milk, passion fruit and pumpkin seeds. If you're looking for something savoury, pop into their secret back garden, where you'll find *L'Hort*: a Catalan-inspired snack bar serving jamon iberico and Spanish tortilla.

Night Rooster

9 *Creative Craft Cocktails*

🏠 Jalan Dewisita 10b (upstairs)

☎ +62 361977733

↖ locavore.co.id/nightrooster

f Night Rooster by Locavore

◎ @thenightrooster

⊘ Mon – Sat, 4pm – 12am
Closed Sun

There isn't a huge amount of good bars in Ubud if you want to drink something slightly more exciting than beer, making *Night Rooster* a special spot. Created by the guys behind *Locavore*, *Night Rooster* is an impressive bar experience, which has reached international acclaim and appreciation. Reflecting the values of its restaurant sisters, *Night Rooster* uses fresh local ingredients to make drinks such as 'the passion just flew away' with passionfruit, mint from their garden, and spiced rum, or 'Jack & Gin' with jackfruit-infused Tanqueray gin, jasmine bitter and mangosteen. The interiors of this place are gorgeous too. I love the black petrified tree trunk tabletops, which I hear were made using trees from chef Eelke's home in the Netherlands. Be sure to chat to head alchemist Raka, who can talk you through his homemade exotic infusions made using combinations of local fruits and spices, and who'll be happy to shake you up a bespoke cocktail.

Ewa Oceanic Art Gallery

10 *Terrific Tribal Adornments*

Bianca Todorov, the founder of this shop, grew up in Papua New Guinea and spent years travelling the remote Sepik River, where, with her family, she met local villagers and began to collect the artworks and artefacts that are so unique to the tribes. She began to incorporate the adornments of the tribes into her personal style, such as wild boar tusks and ancient shell money. This experience inspired her to start *Ewa Jewelry,* a brand steeped in tribal influences. Find half-moon pendants created from Kualia shells adorned with 22K gold details, with the metalwork done by talented local Balinese artisans. Or pick up a Sepik tusk choker made using a reclaimed tusk that has been handed down through generations of New Guinea people. I was lucky enough to interview Bianca (see page 189), while I was in Ubud, as I was so fascinated with her story and the gorgeous pieces she is putting out into the world.

🏠 Jalan Dewi Sita 1

☎ +62 81236835261

🏹 ewaoceanicgallery.com or
ewatribaljewelry.com

✉ info@ewaoceanicgallery.com

📘 Ewa Tribal Jewelry

📷 @ewajewelry

🕐 Mon – Sun 10am - 5pm

Ikat Batik

(11) *Handmade Traditional Textiles*

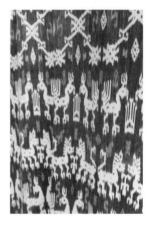

🏠 Jalan Monkey Forest

☎ +62 361975622

↖ ikatbatik.com

✉ info@ikatbatik.com

⊙ @ikatbatik

⊘ Mon – Sun 9am – 9pm

It can be tricky to find the well-hidden *Ikat Batik* shop on busy Monkey Forest Road, so keep your eyes peeled for an indigo-lined walkway leading into an incense-filled courtyard. Indonesia has a rich culture of craftsmen known for their hand-woven textiles, and *Ikat Batik* works to promote and support these communities and help maintain their traditional way of life. The pieces here are hand-spun, hand-dyed, all natural batik from Bali. Pick up samples of hand-dyed fabric to decorate your home. I bought a pale blue ikat piece of fabric, which I used to upholster a bedroom bench, with fabric spare for cushions. The showrooms are styled beautifully too; they have piles of fabulous cushions and big poufs already made up, and rails of blue clothing at the back of the shop.

Gaya Ceramics

12 *Italian-style Ceramics*

🏠 Jalan Raya Sayan 105

☎ +62 361976220

🏹 gayaceramic.com

✉ info@gayaceramic.com

📘 Gaya Ceramic

📷 @gayaceramic

🕐 Mon – Sat 9am – 6pm
Closed Sun

The gorgeous *Gaya Ceramics* is not to be missed if you want the most exquisite and sophisticated tableware for your home. They predominantly specialise in custom handmade collections for big clients such as luxury hotels and restaurants (they export 90% or their wares), but you can buy off-the-shelf items in their retail store here in Ubud. Founded by an Italian couple who originally came to Bali for a holiday 15 years ago, *Gaya* now works with 80 craftsmen on site to hand-throw around 7,000 pieces per month. Italian sophistication meets Balinese craftsmanship is how they describe it. It's fascinating to see the amazing plates, bowls, vases and cups being made in the busy workshop. If you want to try your hand at creating your own pieces, you can sign up for the weekly classes that they hold here in their arts centre, with an in-house instructor to show you the ropes.

Kevala Ceramics

13 *Handcrafted Homewares*

During a meal at *Locavore* I couldn't help but marvel at the beautiful plates, bowls and cups they were using to serve their food on. To my delight I found that they source their tableware locally from *Kevala Ceramics*, and the shop was just across the road! The word 'Kevala' in Sanskrit means perfect, whole and complete, and the ceramics are entirely handmade by local artisans in Bali. The products they sell are stunning and will make any meal you create at home look really fancy. I bought a whole cupboard's worth of plates, vases and bowls to take with me on the plane home. It is amazing value for the quality you get and beats the mass produced factory stuff in the shops. As well as the Ubud branch, you can also stock up at their shop in Seminyak.

Jalan Dewi Sita

+62 3614792532

kevalaceramics.com

Kevala Ceramics

@kevalaceramics

Mon - Sun 9am - 7.30pm

The Yoga Barn

14 *Holistic Healing Hangout*

🏠 Jalan Pengosekan

📞 +62 361971236

🔗 theyogabarn.com

✉️ info@theyogabarn.com

f The Yoga Barn - Bali

📷 @theyogabarn

🕐 Mon - Sun 7am - 9pm

More than simply a space to come and practice your tree pose, *The Yoga Barn* is an action-packed community centre for the spiritually inclined. It's the sort of place where you'll drop in for a session of Vinyasa Flow and then stumble into Tibetan bowl meditation, before sipping on a green juice at the Garden Kafe. This place is so blissful that the toughest decision you will have to make is whether to fill your afternoon with community astrology or Yin Yoga Healing. Centrally located in Ubud town, anyone is welcome to drop into one of *The Yoga Barn's* hourly classes, priced at Rp130k. It's the perfect place to come on your own for a bit of time out, and you can also stay on-site in their guesthouse accommodation if you want to make the most of what's on offer. Be sure to also book yourself in for a marvellous Ayurvedic massage at their spa *Kush*. Go for a 60-minute 'Relaxing Abhyanga Massage' priced at a very reasonable Rp270k a session.

Intuitive Flow

15 *Scenic Yoga Studio*

With panoramic views over the valleys of Ubud and of the volcanoes in the distance, this might just be one of the most scenic studios you'll have the chance to practice yoga in. *Intuitive Flow* is located in the artists' village of Penestanan and is quite off the beaten track so can be hard to find, but it's worth the search and it also generally means that the classes are uncrowded. The atmosphere here is intimate and welcoming. It is a lovely place to come for a morning yoga session, when the morning light floods through the window. Afterwards, pop into the nearby *Yellow Flower Cafe* for fresh juices and organic food. Drop-in yoga classes are Rp120k.

🏠 Jalan Raya Tjampuhan, Penestanan

☎ +62 361977824

↖ intuitiveflow.com

✉ contact@intuitiveflow.com

📘 Intuitive Flow Yoga Studio

🕐 Mon - Sun 7am - 7pm

Hubud

16 *Community Co-Working Space*

While I'm not encouraging you to work while on holiday, if you work remotely or for yourself, there's no better place to do this than Bali. *Hubud* is part of the growing global co-working space movement, and it attracts creative entrepreneurs from all over the world. It really is one of the most incredible places you could call an office, with its breezy bamboo building and everyday scenes like children flying their kites in the field in front of you. The on site cafe, *Living Food Lab*, is slightly more exciting than your average office canteen, offering raw treats, juices and fruit smoothies. There is a strong community aspect to *Hubud*, where members collaborate and help each other, and there's always inspiring events and courses held throughout each month.

🏠 Jalan Monkey Forest, 88X

☎ +62 361978073

↖ hubud.org

✉ team@hubud.org

f Hubud: Ubud coworking
community space

⭕ @hubudbali

$ From $60 per month

Be Bali Stay

17 *Authentic Balinese B&B*

🏠 Banjar Tanggayuda,
Kedewatan, Ubud

☎ +62 8123608079

↖ bebalistay.com or
airbnb.com/rooms/6353317

✉ putu@balifriend.net

⊡ @bebalistay

$ From $150

Be Bali Stay is a wonderful Balinese homestay run by the most lovely local family on their farm. A short drive north of Ubud, the villa is situated in a quiet valley looking over the rice terraces which the family continues to cultivate. The two-bedroom two-story house is spacious and comfortable, with a kitchen and living room area with a daybed, as well as a balcony that runs around it with gorgeous views to the valley. What makes this place so unique are the people that run it; a real Balinese family who can show you their way of life. Be sure to book a cooking lesson with Made, where you'll learn how to prepare traditional Balinese dishes from their lovely open-air kitchen (cooking lessons can be booked by non-guests too). The owner Putu and his family strive to give back to the local community, using proceeds from the villa bookings to pay for English classes for children from the village.

Como Uma Ubud

18 *Charming Contemporary Resort*

If you're looking for a special hotel close to the heart of Ubud, *Como Uma Ubud* is the place to go. The more affordable little sister of the famous *Como Shambhala Estate*, this hotel maintains the same wellness and foodie details that run through the whole of the *Como* brand. The 46-room hotel is stylish, rustic and casual but consciously thought out, with an eye for detail in everything from the bohemian interior design to the fabulous healthy food menu. The rooms are filled with natural light and decorated reflecting Southeast Asian influences, such as cushions made from local batik and ikat textiles and rattan tables and chairs. Some of the villas have pools, or alternatively there's the lovely hotel pool, which rarely feels crowded. Food wise, I loved their Como Shambhala healthy breakfast, with options like quinoa, pear and cinnamon porridge and egg white omelette with kale and roasted tomatoes. The massages here are magnificent – treat yourself to an invigorating Indonesian massage using eucalyptus and peppermint oils.

🏠 Jalan Raya Sanggingan

☎ +62 361972448

🔾 comohotels.com/umaubud

✉ uma.ubud@comohotels.com

📘 Como Hotels & Resorts

📷 @comohotels

💲 From $290

Omah Padi

19 *Beautiful Bamboo Villa*

There are some brilliant villas in and around Ubud, and if you're travelling with a group of friends or family then you can't get much better than *Omah Padi*. The villa is designed to reflect traditional styles, with bamboo buildings and thatched roofs. There are five bedrooms, each with their own tropical bathrooms and an amazing open-air living pavilion. I especially like the remote feel of the villa, with magnificent unspoilt views over the rice paddies (something that's becoming rare the closer you get to central Ubud). If you're with a group, it makes sense to hire a driver who can take you into town for the restaurants, or alternatively it's a quick trip on a bike. There are staff around to help you with anything you need, such as in-villa massages – what a dream!

🏠 Jalan Jukut Paku, Singakerta, Ubud

🖱 airbnb.com/rooms/1531399

💲 From $550

Alam Ubud

20 *Peaceful Jungle Hideaway*

One of the best things about visiting Bali is the choice of wonderful places you can stay for around $100 a night. I stumbled across this gem of a hotel on my first visit to Bali and have been back again and again. Location 9km north of Ubud in the Tagallalang area, *Alam Ubud* is blissfully peaceful and its situation in the valley is beyond beautiful. The hotel is small, with around 20 rooms or 'villas' dotted around the hill. Some come with pools so it's all very private, and you'll often have the main pool to yourself. Yoga classes are held in the valley by the flowing river, and they do fab cooking lessons where you can learn to make local dishes like chicken satay, sambal and nasi goreng.

🏠 Desa Kendran, Tegallalang

☎ +62 8970901009

🖝 alamubudvilla.com

✉ info@alamubudvilla.com

$ From $120

Rumah Hujan

21 *Dreamy Design Villa*

This thoughtfully designed villa just outside of Ubud town centre has jaw-dropping, unrivalled views down into the jungle-like valley. This three-bedroom villa is great for groups, with good lounging and communal areas too. The design is stylish and sophisticated, with European influences mixed in with local flavours (the talented designer also did *Como Uma Ubud* and the *Four Seasons* hotel). The breakfast here is amazing; fresh croissants, bread and jam and delicious coffee. The showstopper is the outdoor seating area, which feels like you're floating above the valley; a perfect spot for a sunset gin and tonic. Living just next door, the lovely owners Stefanie and Max are super helpful in organising everything from bikes to beers, to in-villa yoga and BBQs.

🏠 Jalan Raya Sanggingan

➤ airbnb.com/rooms/19001034

💲 From $500

Passiflora

22 *Dreamy Javanese Joglo*

If you want a totally unique lodging experience in the Ubud area, look no further than the wonderful *Passiflora*. Located in the quiet rice paddy fields in the artists' village of Penestanan, *Passiflora* is a 100-year-old antique wooden joglo. Masterminded by Alejandra, a Bali based Argentine-American architect, who personally visits Java to seek out these beautiful buildings and brings them back piece by piece to be reassembled. Everything about this home — from the carved blue-washed wooden walls, the peaceful position five minutes walk from any road, the lush greenery surrounding it, to the salt water pool — is a total dream. The gorgeous bathroom is outdoors and surrounded by plants, so it's like having a bath in a little jungle. Staff is on hand to make you plates of fruit and toast for breakfast, and they can even organise a spoiling in-joglo massage.

🏠 Penestanan, Ubud

↖ airbnb.com/rooms/58045

⑤ $170

Penestanan Young Artists

23 *Artists' Neighbourhood*

Penestanan is a little village next to Ubud town. It is known as the 'Young Artist's Village' due to the community of artists that formed here during the 1900s. European artists came to Bali and started working alongside local painters where a new style of work was formed. You can still see this genre of painting when visiting local artists, such as the much admired I Ketut Soki. It's a special experience visiting the home and studio of this artist. He has beautiful finished works depicting daily island life: traditional ceremonies, dancing and farming – all illustrated using bold, bright colours. To learn more about this artists' movement, visit the nearby *Neka Art Museum*, which shows a great collection of varying local works with accompanying information.

I Ketut Soki

🏠 Penestanan Kelod

☎ +62 361974370

Neka Art Museum

🏠 Raya Campuhan St.

☎ +62 361975074

🔖 museumneka.com

Celuk Silver Village

 Handcrafted Silver Jewellery

The village of Celuk, 11km south of Ubud, is the centre for silversmiths in Bali. The skills of the local artists have been passed down through generations; most inhabitants of Celuk are part of jeweller families and silversmiths themselves. I suggest you visit the shop *Rama Sita*, which is a wonderful gallery with a workshop on site that promotes the wares of local artists. The items on sale here are some of the highest quality works of craftsmanship you will see. My favourite item was a hand-carved wooden bowl with an intricately designed silver snake wrapped around it – totally unique! If you take a look out the back you can see the talented silversmiths in action, crafting the most beautiful and detailed pieces of art.

Rama Sita

 Rama Sita, Jalan Raya Celuk

 +62 361298054

Guide
I suggest using a driver to visit the artists' villages, as they can be tricky to find. I recommend Putu Arnawa, who is a very knowledgeable Bali guide.

 balifriend.com

 putuarnawa@aol.com

Mas

25 *Creative Wood Carving Village*

Antique Furniture

For those of you that go weak at the knees at the sight of brightly coloured Indonesian doors and think it's perfectly practical to want to sleep in an antique Balinese daybed, I've found just the place for you. Best known for its tradition of woodcarving, Mas is also home to a collection of lovely antique and wooden furniture shops. My favourite store is *Tan Celagi*, which stocks antique joglo furniture sourced from Java. Think 20ft-wide carved wooden walls, turquoise coloured screens and intricately painted tall wooden doors.

Tan Celagi

🏠 Jalan Raya Mas

☎ +62 81392513920

✉ tancelagi@yahoo.com

Mask Making

Wood Carving

Njana Tilem Gallery

🏠 Jalan Raya Mas

☎ +62 361975099

✉ njanatilemgallery@yahoo.co.id

I W Mudana

🏠 Br. Batanancak, Mas

☎ +62 361974549

✉ mudana.master@gmail.com

As the central Ubud stores increasingly hawk mass-produced souvenirs, you'll need to travel to Mas to find the real deal (a short 5km south from Ubud town). The pioneer of the local wood carving scene was a man named Ida Bagus Tilem and you can visit an interesting museum run by his sons called the *Njana Tilem* Gallery, showcasing stunning works representing everyday life in Bali, be it farmers or fishermen, frozen in wood. I also recommend visiting I W Mudana's studio, where you can see Mudana's own contemporary style of carving using irregular shaped wood with twists and holes. He has rooms full of stunning works, known for their spiraling heights and individuality.

If you're looking for a truly special Balinese token to take home with you, I suggest you visit I Wayan Muka's mask-making studio to pick up one of his unique creations. Like most craftsmen on the island, his skills have been passed down through generations. You can see the whole process, from the blocks of wood he uses to carve the faces, to the beautiful finished products displayed on the walls. The amount of time and skill that goes into making a mask is unbelievable; one piece can use up to 350 coats of paint to make it a finished product. Read my interview with this talented man on page 205.

I Wayan Muka

🏠 Br Batancak, Mas

☎ +62 361974530

✉ spiritofmask@yahoo.com

Tampak Siring

 Curious Carvings & Terrific Temples

Bone Carving village

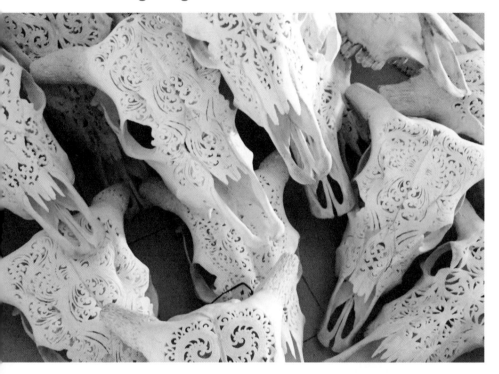

You may see examples of bull and buffalo skull carvings appearing in shops on your travels around Bali, but I suggest making a trip up to the specialist 'Bone Carving' village of Tampak Siring to see the masters at work and to support them at the source. The quiet village streets are dotted with storefronts where you can meet the bone carvers themselves. Ask kindly and they may let you into their workshop behind their store. Visiting the artisans themselves means that you have a greater choice of what's on offer, and most do custom orders so you can come with your own design to have hand carved into the skulls. Shops offer varying prices, but as a benchmark look to pay Rp500k for a piece. I'd recommend the shop *Ida Bagus Tantra* for good quality and price. Nearby is the sacred 'Tirta Empul Temple' famous for its holy water, so you can also stop off to see this while you're here.

Ida Bagus Tantra

 Br. Penaka, Tampak Siring

Gunung Kawi

After visiting Tampak Siring a few times, mainly to stock up on carved cow heads to bring home for friends, it was only recently that I came across the magnificent temple, *Gunung Kawi*. Unlike better-known temples with hoards of people, (like the tourist-trap Tanah Lot!), *Gunung Kawi* had only a handful of visitors when I went along early one morning. Located half an hour's drive north of central Ubud, *Gunung Kawi* is a magnificent collection of temples that were first built in the 11th century, after Hindus migrated from Java to Bali. Commissioned by the then king of Bali, Udayana, each temple represents members of his family. The temples, carved into the rocks with green foliage growing around them, make you feel like you've uncovered some mystical jungle sanctuary. The temple here is still in use, so you'll likely see local people here doing ceremonies and going about their daily life. Be sure to visit early in the morning when it's cooler; as there are quite a few steps to walk down to get to the temple, an activity that can get hot!

Tampak Siring, Gianyar

Klungkung

 Authentic Balinese Bazaar & Buildings

Klungkung market

🏠 Jalan Puputan, 7,
Semarapura Kangin,
Klungkung

🕐 Mon – Sun 9am – 5pm

Klungkung market is a really local and authentic textiles market. Located in the town of Semarapura (about 22km or 50 mins east of Ubud), it is mainly visited by Balinese people. Come here to pick up a traditional sarong in any colour you can imagine. Note, as this is a very local market, the stall holders here won't speak any English, so you'll need to brush up on your Bahasa if you want to chat to them. They have lovely ikat textiles and sarongs in rich purples, oranges and blues. The beautiful pieces here come directly from the weavers and take a huge amount of time and skill to make, so don't be alarmed if you think the prices are quite high (these aren't the types of sarongs that are sold by beach hawkers for a few dollars). For textile geeks, look out for the single and double ikat pieces in deep natural colours, using dyes from root, bark and leaves. My personal favourite are the embroidered songket fabrics hand-woven with silk.

Kertha Gosa Pavilion

After your visit to *Klungkung market*, wander over to the interesting *Kertha Gosa Pavilion*, a marvellous example of Balinese architecture and art. Originally built in the early 18th century, *Kertha Gosa* was formerly used as a court of law. This was where the king would sit with his ministers to discuss matters of justice in the kingdom. The ceilings are ornately painted in reds and golds with the story of Bhima Swarga, a Hindu epic from the Mahabharata tale. The painters who worked on the ceiling were from the local village of Kamasan, a place of cultural importance as the traditional styles of modern Balinese painting comes from the Kamasan style, which in turn takes its influence from ancient Java. As well as the stories, the paintings also show Balinese daily life, such as people trading at the markets, and the odd tiger, which used to reside on the island.

 Jalan Kenanga, 11, Semarapura Kelod, Klungkung

🕐 Mon – Sun 8am – 5pm

133

Mount Batur

 Volcano Views

Mount Batur is a 1,700m high active volcano in the north east of Bali. Located 35km north of Ubud, the scenic journey there takes around an hour to drive, passing orchards of mandarin orange trees and piles of fruit for sale on the sides of the road. Head towards the highland village of Kintamani, which sits on the rim of the Batur caldera, where you can see the most stunning views of Mount Batur and Lake Batur. There are numerous cafes with viewing decks that you can stop at to have a drink and enjoy the scenery. A popular activity is the trek to the summit of Mount Batur at sunrise: a two-hour climb that starts at around 2am and can be organised with a guide. I definitely recommend a trip here any time of the day to see one of Bali's most beautiful spots.

Getting here
From Ubud, head 35km north towards the village of Kintamani.

Bali Silent Retreat

29 *Transformative & Restorative Sanctuary*

It's difficult to define the *Bali Silent Retreat* as it doesn't fit into a box of yoga or meditation retreat; it's so much more than that. My boyfriend jokes that the ironic thing about the silent retreat is that afterwards, I simply could not stop talking about it to anyone and everyone, urging them they must go. Nestled on the foothills of the sacred Mount Batu Karu volcano and surrounded by rice fields and jungle, the place makes you feel exceptionally close and appreciative of nature. This off the grid eco-sanctuary allows you to spend time reflecting and restoring yourself, without any of the distractions of modern life (no devices or electronics allowed). Days start before dawn with guided meditation and gentle yoga asana. The food here is outstanding. Using solely plant-based ingredients created by New Earth Cooking, it's enough to make anyone go vegan. What I thought was so great about this retreat is that it's so inclusive, meaning anyone can afford to go here. Whether you want to spend more on a luxurious bungalow or are on a budget and want a simple private room, the emphasis is on providing this experience to everyone. I can't wait to come back.

🏠 Banjar Mongan, Penatahan, Penebel, Tabanan Regency

🏹 balisilentretreat.com

✉️ bsrbookings@balisilentretreat.com

📷 @balisilentretreat

💲 $40 for single room, $90 for a bungalow

Balian

 Volcanic Black-Sand Village

Balian Beach

I love the atmosphere at Balian beach, with its jet-black, mesmerising volcanic sand, which feels all the more moody when a storm is about to set in. Located to the west of the island where tourist numbers are fewer, Balian is quieter and a lot more laid-back than some of the more popular beach spots in Bali. Popular with surfers, there are a few little cafes and surfboard rental places on the beach. If surfing is not your thing, the beach is lovely for long walks with literally nothing on the horizon for miles. Grab a coconut or green juice at *Pondok Pitaya* and enjoy the views over the beach.

 Jalan Pantai Balian, West Selemadeg, Tabanan Regency

Matekap Lodge

I stumbled across *Matekap Lodge* near Balian purely by chance. I wanted to find somewhere to break up the journey from Canggu to the *Bali Silent Retreat* near Penebel, and luckily *Matekap Lodge* had availability for the night. When I stayed here there was only one lovely villa (although I believe another is in the plans), so I could enjoy the magnificent views of the rice fields and the deserted black sandy beach all to myself. When people think about Bali they imagine tranquil vistas, but in reality these are growing increasingly harder to find, making this place such a great discovery. I only stayed one night here but I could have easily spent at least four or five days enjoying the soothing sounds of the waves from the huge wooden emperor size bed, or sitting reading a pile of books on the gorgeous veranda.

🏠 Balian, West Selemadeg, Tabanan Regency

↖ airbnb.com/rooms/16344634

Nusa Lembongan

Beautiful Beaches and Wild Waves

A cluster of islands situated off the south east coast of Bali, **Nusa Lembongan** and its sisters **Nusa Ceningan** and **Nusa Penida** are a quieter and more rustic alternative to mainland Bali. Nusa Lembongan, which can be reached by a 30-minute boat ride from the town of Sanur, is the more developed of the three, with more choice of accommodation and restaurants.

Roads are bumpy, and there aren't any cars bar a few transport trucks used by resorts. Travellers meander around the islands of Lembongan and Ceningan on mopeds: the best way to get around.

The main activities on these islands are snorkelling and surfing. Days are laid back, simple and always with a dose of adventure. Beach hopping is a must. It is made all the more idyllic as you slowly pass by seaweed strewn on the roadside drying under the sun and wooden fishing boats floating in turquoise waters.

The beaches on the island are beautiful, although looks can be deceiving — be careful of the currents and avoid stepping into some waters altogether. What you'll see is your typical tropical island scenes. Willowy palm trees and rugged rocks frame cream-coloured sands.

Nusa Lembongan and its sister islands are rougher around the edges compared to their more popular counterpart. Don't expect fine dining; instead park up on the waterfront at a local Indonesian warung with a smoky grill of fresh snapper with sambal sauce, rice and chicken satay. Nusa Lembongan is best for a short trip; I'd say two or three days would do.

NUSA LEMBONGAN

TO
BALI

Sandy Bay Beach Club

1 *Scenic Beach Restaurant*

This all-day dining hangout has the most scenic setting on Sunset Beach, which can be found on the south west of Nusa Lembongan Island. *Sandy Bay Beach Club* is a stylishly rustic and laid-back restaurant and bar, serving up crowd-pleasing grub like burgers and BBQ grilled seafood. It's a lovely place to come for lunch, where you can wander on the white sand before settling in for a long and lazy eating session. They have a good selection of wines and fruit cocktails on their menu too. As the name of the beach suggests, it's a gorgeous spot for sunset, where the falling sun glistens on the wild waves. *Sandy Bay* also has a boutique filled with bikinis and summer dresses, and there's a spa for post-lunch pampering.

🏠 Sunset Beach, Nusa Lembongan

☎ +62 82897005656

↖ sandybaylembongan.com

✉ tbc@sandybaylembongan.com

f Sandy Bay Beach Club

⊘ Mon - Sun 8am - 10pm

Villa Voyage

2 *Beachfront Party Pad*

It can be hard to find nice accommodation on Nusa Lembongan, so if you want comfort and space I'd always suggest a villa. When you gather a group of friends together even the most luxurious of pads can be affordable. *Villa Voyage* must be one of the best, and with five bedrooms it works out at a reasonable $100 per head if you have a full house, and this includes staff and a chef. The villa is located right on the beautiful Sunset Beach, neighbouring *Sandy Bay Beach Club*. The design is barefoot luxury; all bedrooms have en-suite bathrooms and a contemporary safari chic vibe. There are some other lovely villas surrounding this beach – have a look at the three-bedroom *Island House* next door if you want something slightly smaller.

Villa Voyage

🏹 villavoyagebali.com

$ From $995 per night

Island House

🏹 nusalembonganvillas.com

$ From $300 per night

Dream Beach

3 *White Sand Wonderland*

Just around the corner from Sunset Beach is another one of Nusa Lembongan's picture-postcard scenes – Dream Beach. Quiet and uncrowded, this beauty spot attracts a handful of travellers in the know. The soft sand is an idyllic cream colour and the water a dazzling aqua hue. I was lured in for a dip by the tempting ocean colours, but be warned that the current is strong so swimming isn't advised (I quickly got out!). There's a casual café by the beach for lunch. Go upstairs to the top deck where they have comfy day beds perfect for an afternoon spent getting stuck into your holiday read, with stunning aerial views over Dream Beach. If you want to stay on the beach, there is a sprinkling of simple Balinese lumbung huts metres from the sand for a no-frills sleeping experience.

 Dream Beach,
Nusa Lembongan

Mushroom Bay

4 *Sunset Spot*

Mushroom Bay on the west of Nusa Lembongan has calmer waters compared to its neighbouring beaches. The plus side of this is that it's swimmer friendly although you'll need to time your visit to the beach right. During the day boats full of visitors descend to do sporting activities on its placid waters, so come here past 3pm when it's lovely and quiet again. The vibe is peaceful and relaxed, with a mix of families and couples propped up on beanbags on the sand, ready to admire the stunning sunset that falls on the water on the bay. There's a bamboo structured restaurant *Hai Bar & Grill* where you can get a glass of wine, a cocktail and simple dishes like pizza and calamari. Come to Mushroom Bay for a late afternoon laze around.

Mushroom Bay,
Nusa Lembongan

Seaweed Farmers

5 *Local Life*

Hop on a bike and head to the most southern point of Nusa Lembongan where you will find a bright yellow suspension bridge that connects to Nusa Ceningan (Nusa Lembongan's smaller and quieter neighbour). When you start your journey around this island, one of the first things you will notice is the abundance of green seaweed that has been harvested and is lying out on sheets of tarpaulin on the roadside, drying under the blazing sun. While Bali has its rice, Ceningan has its seaweed, and this has traditionally been the island's main industry. It's nice to stop and see what people are up to, and it's interesting to see a different side to what the locals do which isn't about tourism. I found those I approached to be warm, smiley and friendly. In fact, a couple of ladies I went up to couldn't stop laughing (probably at me).

Getting here
From Nusa Lembongan, head south and look for the yellow bridge that links to Nusa Ceningan. You will find the seaweed farmers all along the coastal roads.

Blue Lagoon

6 *Perilous Beauty Spot*

Make your way by bike to the south west of Nusa Ceningan Island, where you will find the beautiful Blue Lagoon. It may sound like a serene swimming spot, but don't be fooled; although lovely to look at, Blue Lagoon is a wild and treacherous rocky cove with bright blue waves crashing fiercely against limestone walls. There's a cliff edge from which to view this natural beauty spot, but be careful as there are no barriers. Daredevil travellers used to navigate the craggy path around the lagoon to do cliff jumping, although thankfully this activity has since stopped. Blue Lagoon is a magnificent site to simply sit and admire the powerful waves smashing against the shoreline, a striking albeit potentially dangerous situation.

Getting here
From Nusa Lembongan, head south and look for the yellow bridge that links to Nusa Ceningan. Turn right and head along the coastal road. Blue Lagoon is located on the south west of the island.

Secret Beach

7 *Deserted and Rugged Shoreline*

Nestled in a bay on the south of Nusa Ceningan is the often deserted Secret Beach. Like many of the beaches around these islands, the currents are strong and the water unsafe to swim in, but it sure is lovely to look at. There's a narrow strip of biscuit-coloured sand with pieces of driftwood washed up on the shore and a line of thick green shrubs edging behind it. Waves sweep the beach and blast the chunks of rocks embedded into the sand. Dig your bare feet into the soft sand and stand there while the foam-crested waves flow around your legs. Secret Beach is hidden away, so you'll likely be its only visitors. When finding the beach, look out for *Villa Trevally*, which is the small resort next to it. You probably wouldn't want to spend too much time here as there isn't any shade, but it's worth a stop off to admire this beautiful beach.

Getting here

Secret Beach is located on the south west of the island, not far from Blue Lagoon. Look out for *Villa Trevally*, which is the resort next to the beach.

Crystal Bay Beach

8 *Remote Island Life*

A visit to Nusa Penida is much like stepping onto an island that time forgot. The island is best reached by taking a long-armed, wooden outrigger boat from Nusa Lembongan, and the journey takes around 30-40 minutes. The waters at Crystal Bay have become popular with snorkellers and divers attracted to the active underwater world. You can come ashore and step onto its beach, where you will find a distinctly tropical scene. Tall palm trees flank a thin strip of sugary white sand, with colourful boats propped up on the shore. The island is simple, and the locals are friendly. Women spend their mornings washing their clothes in the shallow river, young children splash around and slow cows graze on the green grass. There's a true desert island feel to this place. It is definitely a good half-day trip, with a combination of snorkelling and beach.

Getting here

From Nusa Lembongan, you can organise someone to take you on a boat over to Crystal Bay at Nusa Penida. The journey takes around 30-40 minutes, and the water can be choppy!

Lombok & Gili Islands

Picture-Perfect Island Escapes

35kms east of Bali is the lovely island of **Lombok**. While Bali might get most of the attention from visitors, Lombok is the quiet and unassuming neighbour blessed with bountiful natural beauty.

The channel that lies between Bali and Lombok indicates The Wallace Line; the bio-geographical boundary that marks the transitional zone between Asia and Australia. When arriving in Lombok from Bali you'll notice the drier, more arid landscape. Thick jungle-like flora is replaced by dry grassy knolls, and the birds and animals that reside here are closer in relation to their Australian counterparts than Asian species.

Those who live on Lombok are called the Sasak people. They share a similar language and ancestry with the Balinese, although the Sasak are mainly Muslim, whereas the Balinese are mostly Hindu.

Off the Lombok coast are the charming Gili Islands ('Gili' simply means 'small island' in Sasak), which provide blissful escapes. My happy place is **Gili Asahan**, a tiny island located off the southwest shoreline of Lombok. Not as well know as the Gili islands in the north, Gili Asahan is a special discovery, with gorgeous beaches and comfortable accommodation. Next on the list is **Gili Meno**, a romantic island retreat that's quiet and relaxing. **Gili Air**, its slighter larger neighbour, has got a bit more going on, so is great for those looking for a bit more life and soul.

Getting between Lombok and Bali is easy, with boats making the journey over the channel throughout the day, as well as plenty of short flights between the islands' airports.

GILI ISLANDS

11 10 16
12 15
9 13 14 6

7

← TO BALI

GILI ASAHAN

8

SELONG BELANAK BEACH

2
1
4

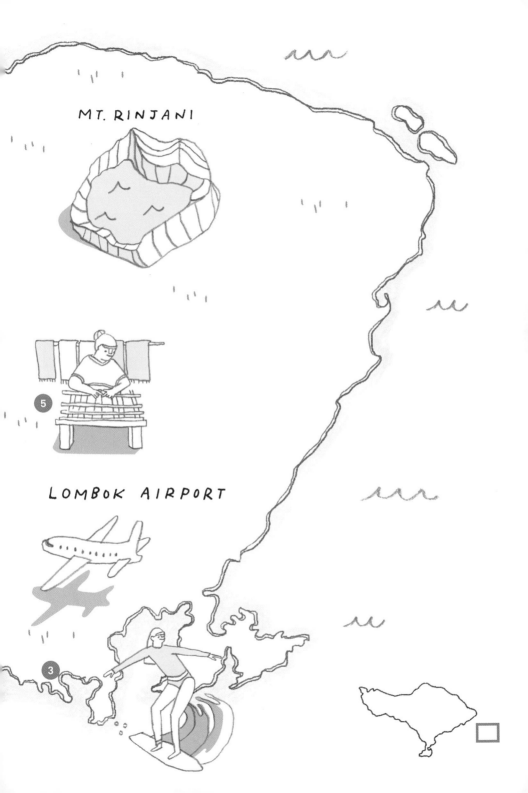

MT. RINJANI

LOMBOK AIRPORT

Sempiak Villas

1 *Villas with a View*

Sempiak Villas is an intimate boutique hotel with six rooms, and is the only accommodation on this stretch of paradise (for now!). With each villa looking out over the stunning sugary crescent of Selong Belanak Beach, finding this hotel and its idyllic location felt a bit like uncovering a well-guarded secret. Along with two friends, I stayed in Villa Okep, which has one main bedroom and a small loft room, with a kitchen and a large living room. Standing on the villa veranda, there are breathtaking panoramic views across the bay. We were right next to the delightful pool too. Breakfast on the beach was a real treat as we sipped on fresh mango juice and local coffee with our feet buried in the sand. Conveniently, *Sempiak Villas* is an easy 20-minute taxi ride away from Lombok airport. Activities include swimming in the sea and pool, surfing and massages – bliss!

🏠 Jalan Datuk Lopan,
Selong Belanak, Lombok

↖ sempiakvillas.com

✉ sempiakvillas@gmail.com

📷 @sempiakvillas

$ From $98

Selong Belanak Beach

2 *Stunning Sandy Bay*

Travellers to Indonesia are spoilt for choice when it comes to beautiful beaches. But Selong Belanak Beach in the south of Lombok has to be one of the best. The crystal-turquoise water is perfect for swimming in, and beginner surfers can hire a board from one of the surf shacks lining the shore. I loved how old-fashioned this part of the island feels. I saw farmers wearing sarongs leading their herd of cows along the beach each day, while an old lady walked along with colourful tin bowls of freshly caught fish. The beach is long, so you can always find a spot for yourself. For drinks and snacks, you can visit the *Laut Biru Bar & Restaurant* (part of *Sempiak Villas*), for juices, beers and lunches.

 Selong Belanak, Lombok

Tanjung Aan Beach

3 *Charming Coastal Scene*

Located on the south coast of Lombok, 5km east of Kuta, Tanjung Aan is a picture-postcard beach with piercing-blue sea and soft white sand. After following a bumpy road, you'll end up at this simple beach, with only a few wooden shacks dotted on the sand. Bring your own towel and settle in for a sunbathing session. The water is generally calm, making it lovely for a refreshing swim. There are hills beside the bay, which are worth climbing to get a gorgeous view of the surrounding area, especially at sunset. Tanjung Aan can get popular at the weekends, so time your trip mid-week if possible. Note that there are no proper restaurants here so it's best to come for a morning dip before jumping back on your bike to continue your island exploration.

 Pantai Tanjung Aan, Lombok

Mawun Beach

 Beautiful Bay

Pantai Mawun, Lombok

Situated on the coast between Selong Belanak and Kuta, Mawun is a calm and tranquil bay flanked by tall grassy headlands. Mawun is small and low-key, and is a perfect spot to come later in the afternoon for a cooling swim and an ice-cold Bintang beer. Bring your own sarongs to lie on, and spend an hour or so relaxing on the soft sand. Walk up the beach, and spot colourful painted blue and green fishing boats on the shore. Not much in the way of facilities - soak up the simple life while sipping on a freshly picked coconut and listening to the soothing sounds of the waves.

Sukarara Weaving Village

5 *Traditional Lombok Textiles*

Weaving brightly coloured traditional cloth, or 'songket', is a daily activity done by the Sasak people of Lombok. It is said that women are required to have this skill before they are to be married. The village of Sukarara is a centre for this custom, where you'll find women who work tirelessly to produce these intricate pieces. Sitting on mats and using old-style wooden weaving equipment, they will spend a whole month working eight hours a day to produce a single two-metre piece of fabric. While the prices here can be considered high compared to the machine made sarongs sold by beach hawkers, the fabric here is a labour of love, made using skills passed down through the generations. In my opinion, this makes the fabric seem quite reasonably priced. Pick up vibrant fabrics in rich reds, grassy greens and peachy oranges to bring back to decorate your home.

 Sukarara, Jonggat, Lombok

Sire Beach

6 *Serene Beach*

In the north of Lombok you'll find the peaceful and pretty Sire Beach, with views reaching to the Gili Islands. The curved bay creates calm waters, perfect for a relaxing swim or a snorkelling session in the shallow waters. Spot fishermen wading out to sea catching fish on a rod, with Mount Agung volcano on neighbouring Bali as a backdrop. To enjoy the beach to its fullest, you can stay at the terrific *Tugu Hotel*, which has daybeds nestled on the sand, or if you're in a group there's the stylish *Sira Beach House*, also directly on this gorgeous stretch of coastline. The beach is 5km long, with a few public parts open with local warungs and snack bars.

⌂ Pantai Sire, Lombok

Tugu Hotel

7 *Cultural Indonesian Experience*

Tugu Hotel is not only one of the most beautiful places to stay in Lombok, but also a complete cultural experience. An antithesis to the cookie cutter style of chain hotels, staying at the *Tugu* feels more like you're a visitor at a wonderful curated museum. The *Tugu's* founder, Anhar Setjadibrata, is the owner of the biggest collection of Indonesian fine art and antiquities in the country, which he displays and shares with the lucky guests at his hotels. Interestingly, the rooms are made from original houses salvaged from the colonial era, with details such as tall antique doors, huge wooden four-poster beds, and deep copper bathtubs. The hotel is located directly on the stunning Sire Beach, so you can alternate between a dip in the luscious turquoise pool and the calm pale blue sea. The spa here is outstanding. Named *Hening Swarga*, which means 'heavenly slice', the treatment room is in an open-air temple facing the Indian Ocean, using ancient herbal and spiritual treatments.

🏠 Jalan Pantai Sire

☎ +62 3706120111

🠶 tuguhotels.com/hotels/lombok

✉ lombok@tuguhotels.com

📘 Tugu Hotels

📷 @tuguhotels

💲 From $220

Gili Asahan

Secret Gili Island

(8) Gili Asahan Eco Lodge

If you're looking to get as close to a castaway island experience as possible, then look no further than the wonderful *Gili Asahan Eco Lodge*. Not to be confused with the better-known Gili Islands in the northwest of Lombok, Gili Asahan is one of the 'secret Gilis', a group of undiscovered islands located off Lombok's southwest coast. This small eco-resort has a handful of charming bungalows a stone's throw away from an impossibly beautiful beach. Created by a lovely couple who are both architects, and who live in Bali, the resort has been built using local materials with details such as daybeds made from driftwood and traditional thatched roofs. We spent our days swimming off the beach in the bright blue sea, beach-combing for pretty shells, snorkelling above an untouched reef, watching the sunset from on top of the hill and singing songs around the bonfire in the evening. It was such a unique experience!

🏠 Gili Asahan, Lombok

☎ +62 81339604779

↖ giliasahan.com

✉ info@giliasahan.com

f Gili Asahan – eco lodge

⊙ @giliasahanecolodge

$ From $75

162

Gili Asahan Surroundings

A wonderful experience to enjoy while staying on Gili Asahan Island is the amazing snorkelling that can be done either directly off the beach or nearby around the other 'secret Gili' islands. We took a traditional wooden outrigger boat to the nearby islands of Gili Ringgit and Gili Layar to see what was going on through the lens of a snorkelling mask. Delightful coral with vibrant marine life surrounds these undeveloped islands. Dozens of brightly coloured fish could be seen meandering around the rocks and other fish forming shiny blue silvery walls. The lovely people at *Gili Asahan Eco Lodge* can arrange boat trips and snorkelling equipment for a fun afternoon trip.

 Gili Asahan, Lombok

Gili Meno

9 *Romantic Island Escape*

The Gili Islands are located in a cluster off the northwest coast of Lombok, with Gili Meno being the smallest of the three. The island has managed to maintain the low-key, relaxed island vibe that people imagine when thinking about these picturesque islands. Quiet and the least developed, Gili Meno is popular with couples and honeymooners and people looking for a peaceful escape. With only a few accommodation choices dotted around the coast of this little island, it doesn't feel crowded and attracts those who would rather read a novel than jive in beach bars til the early hours. The beaches are clean and the water is a beautiful aquamarine hue. There's superb snorkelling and diving around the island, and you can spot turtles swimming casually near the Gili Meno wall. Don't come here expecting the same food scene as Bali. There are a few food options at warungs and western snack bars such as *Seri Resort* and *Mallia's Bungalows* where people gather for coconuts and beers. If you are staying in a villa, I suggest organising your own BBQ with fresh fish and shellfish caught locally for a tasty dinner.

Getting here

From Bali, there are a few boat companies that arrange transport to the Gili islands. They also arrange your taxi transfers from your accommodation to the port. I went with Ekajaya fast boat from Padangbai that have a 9am and 1pm departure times from Bali. Expect to pay around 900,000 Rp ($63) for a return trip. The journey takes a few hours door to door. From Lombok, the Gili Islands are a short 30-minute boat-trip.

➤ baliekajaya.com

✉ reservation@baliekajaya.com

Crusoe House

10 *Barefoot Luxury Lodge*

Sister villa of *The Island Houses* in Seminyak, the absolutely breath-taking *Crusoe House* is one of the most unique and special places that you can stay at in Indonesia. Located directly on the beach on the east coast of Gili Meno with views to the sea, the house is designed in a sensitive, traditional style with thatched roofs and sandy coloured walls. With four bedrooms, it is great for groups and families. The rooms are stylishly furnished with French linens on comfy beds, vintage chairs and colourful rustic cabinets. Start your morning with a swim in the stunning swimming pool, which has been subtly built into the sand and is surrounded by pink and orange bougainvillea flowers. I love the small thoughtful touches, such as chic straw sunhats laid out on the sun loungers, delicious smelling soaps in the bathrooms and baskets filled with snorkels, goggles and fins and off-road bikes for exploring the island. When can I come back?

🏠 Gili Meno, North Lombok

↖ theislandhouses.com

✉ bookings@theislandhouses.com

📷 @theislandhouses

💲 From $540

Villa Pulau Cinta

11 *Sumptuous Seaside Retreat*

On the west coast of Gili Meno is the tastefully designed *Villa Pulau Cinta*, which has been crafted from a 200-year-old joglo house sourced from Java. There are six-ensuite bedrooms and spacious and comfortable communal areas. Useful to know is that the bedrooms can be rented individually if there's just two of you, or the villa as a whole if you're in a big group. There are some seriously luxurious touches, such as the cinema room with a four-metre screen (for those cosy, stormy evenings). With quality accommodation limited in Gili Meno, this is a great choice for any size of group. They have a villa manager and staff on site, including an in-house chef who can whip up both Western and Asian dishes. The location of the house is pretty idyllic – the blue pool seamlessly merges into the ocean, which you can hop, skip and jump into for a snorkelling session.

🏠 Gili Meno, North Lombok

🔝 villapulaucinta.com

✉️ escape@villapulaucinta.com

⭕ @villapulaucinta

💲 From $218 per room

Gili Air

12 *Stunning Seaside Sanctuary*

Gili Air, the middle-sized Gili Island, has the best of both worlds; quiet and serene spaces where you might not see another soul for a few hours, as well as laid-back beach bars dotted on the coast where you can wind down in the evening with a few fruity cocktails. If Gili Meno is perfect for honeymooners and couples, I'd say Gili Air is good for groups of friends or even solo travellers. While the island has slightly more going on than Gili Meno, it doesn't have that over-development feel that Gili Trawangan has sadly fallen victim to. Like all of the Gili Islands, cars aren't allowed, so the modes of transport are horse and cart and bicycle. As well as sunset beach bars, there is a good choice of restaurants and cafes, with anything from burritos at *The Mexican Kitchen*, fresh seafood sizzling on BBQ grills at *Zipp Bar*, smoothies bowls with avo on toast at *Gili Bliss* or margherita pizza at *Classico Italiano*.

Getting here
Same transport as for Gili Meno
(see page 164)

Manusia Dunia Green Lodge

13 *Intimate Island B&B*

Run by two French sisters, *Manusia Dunia Green Lodge* is a lovely little six-bedroom boutique B&B located on the quiet western side of Gili Air. There's a good-sized pool with a few sun loungers, surrounded by a thoughtful garden bursting with bright-pink blooms. The lodge has been designed using traditional Indonesian techniques and materials, and they've decorated the place with love and care, from the antique furniture to the comfortable chairs and lovely table linens laid out at breakfast. Set back slightly from the beach, you have a view of the sea from the terrace, which also has little nooks for reading and hammocks strung from post to post, with piles of books left from previous travellers to while away the afternoons.

↖ manusiadunia.com

⊙ @giliairmanusiadunia

$ Rooms from $67

Slow Villas

14 *Secluded Villas & Spa*

↖ slowgiliair.com

◎ @slowgiliair

$ Villas from $200

Also on the quiet western side of the island is the stylish *Slow Villas*. There are 10 luxurious private villas, with either one or two bedrooms. The villas are on the pricier side for Gili Air, although what you're paying for is the privacy; each villa has its own pool and terrace set amid a coconut garden. Villas also have small kitchens, and a personal cook is available to make you a romantic dinner. Also part of the small resort is *Slow Spa*, a serene Japanese-style space built using bamboo. Book an evening massage or spruce yourself up with a pedicure; non-guests can book spa treatments too.

Mowies

15 *Beachside Bungalows & Cafe*

If you're looking for cheap and cheerful accommodation, or a cafe with a view, then *Mowies* is a good choice. Looking over the calm pale blue waters on the 'sunset side' of the island, *Mowies* is a laid-back beachside spot with comfortable but rustic ocean-view beach hut bungalows. There's also a fab cafe that's open to everyone, serving delicious breakfasts, juices and kombucha (go for the dragonfruit and banana with basil smoothie). A great place for sunset, come here late in the afternoon for a cocktail or two.

mowiesbargiliair.com

@mowiesgiliair

Rooms from $50

Pachamama

16 *Vegan Cuisine & Bohemian Villa*

If you're into healthy, vegan grub then *Pacahamama* cafe is the top spot. Devour dishes like zucchini pesto pasta, tempeh nasi bowls and roast eggplant, or sweets that use raw and gluten free ingredients. You can also stay at the bohemian-styled *Pachamama* villa next door. The spacious villa is beautifully decorated, with two double bedrooms, sleeping four. There's a cool plunge pool and outdoor terrace, and of course you can get all your yummy meals provided by the cafe. The location is slightly inland, so set back from the beach, but it's only a few minutes walk to the shore, where you can enjoy amazing snorkelling and swimming.

➤ pachamamagiliair.com or
airbnb.com/rooms/7506968

📷 @pachamamagiliair

$ Villa from $180

Komodo Islands

Archipelago for Adventurers

Located in-between the larger islands of Sumbawa and Flores, the Komodo National Park, known as the 'Komodo Islands', feels like its own magical world, only a short flight away from Bali (500 kms west).

The first thing people think of is of course the Komodo dragons, large lizards that reside exclusively on this collection of islands. But really that isn't the main draw. Komodo Islands is in the centre of the 'Coral Triangle', a 6 million km^2 area covering Indonesia, Malaysia, the Philippines, Papua New Guinea, the Solon Islands and Timor Leste, a region that contains the highest diversity of coral reef species in the world.

Therefore, to just see the dragons would be a wasted trip indeed. For travellers venturing to these islands, both divers and snorkellers, there is an abundance of stunning marine life to enjoy. The islands are natural and undeveloped, with the main mode of transport and accommodation being on a boat. This means that the islands feel untouched, and as a visitor, you feel like an intrepid explorer on your own East Indonesian adventure.

The National Park is comprised of three large islands: Komodo, Padar and Rinca as well as a couple of hundred smaller islands and countless little islets in a 2,000 km^2 area. Also known as the 'Amazon of the seas', it was recognised as a UNESCO World Heritage Site in 1991. In the Komodo National Park specifically there are more than 1,000 species of tropical fish and more than 260 species of coral.

Similarly to Lombok, the land here is dry and arid, with grassy headlands and calm piercing-blue coves creating gorgeous dramatic panoramic scenes.

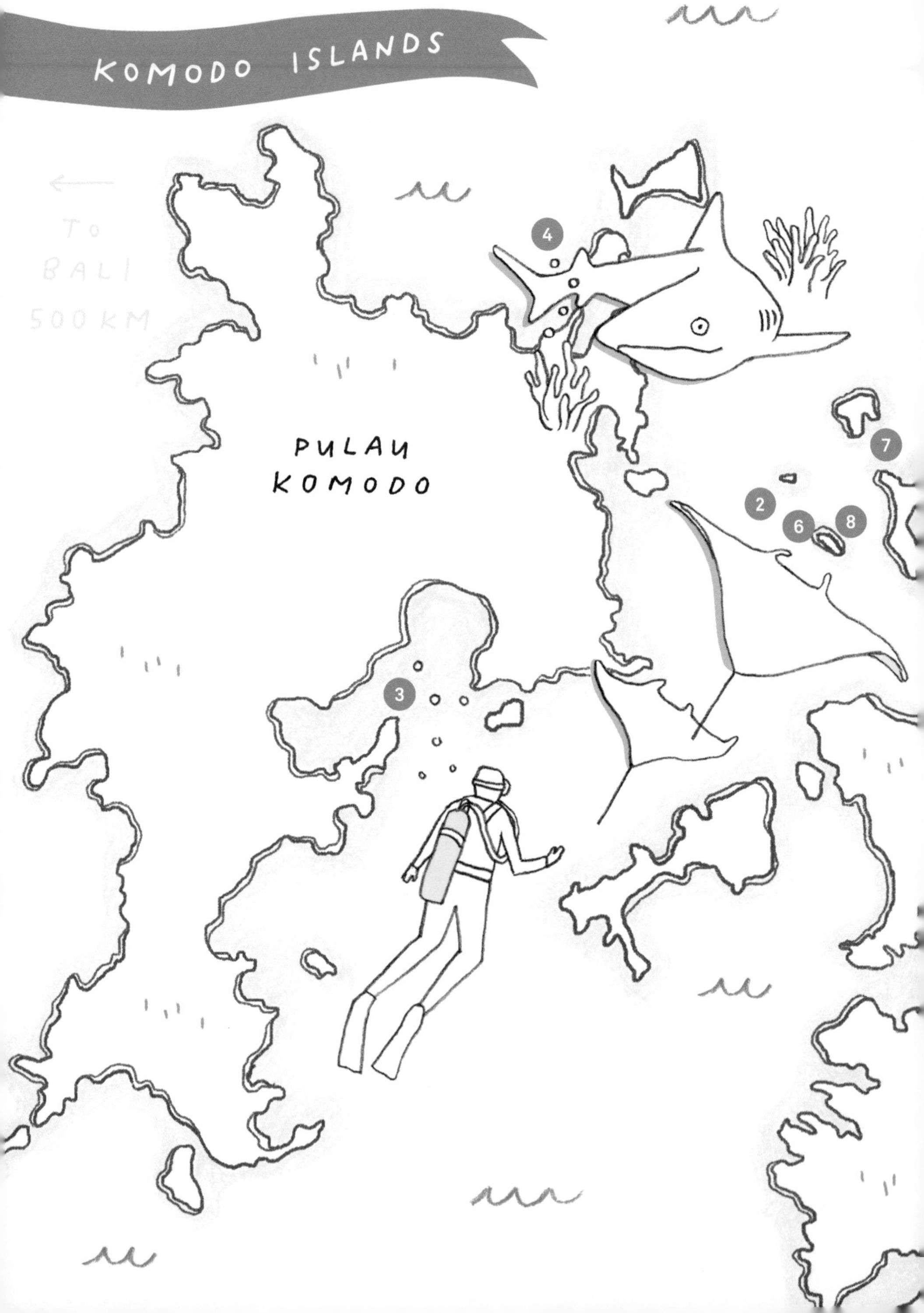

KOMODO ISLANDS

← TO
BALI
500 KM

PULAU
KOMODO

4

2

6

8

7

3

Getting to Komodo Islands

- The easiest way to get to the Komodo Islands is to fly from Denpasar (DPS) in Bali to Labuanbajo (LBJ) in Flores. When flying from Bali you will need to go to the domestic airport

- Flights are direct

- The duration of the flight is around one hour

- Flights cost around $100 return

- There are around eight flights a day from DPS to LBJ with the airlines: Wings Air, Garuda Indonesia and Nam Air

- It is best to stay the night before in Bali and fly to Labuanbajo early the next day so that you arrive in the morning to board your boat. For example, I took the 8am flight from Bali and the 4pm return flight from Labuanbajo with Wings Air

- The airport at LBJ is a convenient 20-min drive to the port from where you will get your boat

Things to note

Medical Care: You will need to purchase additional travel insurance that covers any risks associated with diving including evacuation, as there is no recompression chamber in the Komodo area, with the closest one being in Bali. I paid $60 for 'comprehensive insurance' with AXA for two people for our four-day trip.

Diving Certificate: You will need to have at least a *PADI Open Water Diver* certificate, or the equivalent before diving in Komodo Islands. Diving isn't essential though – some people decide to just snorkel and have a whale of a time.

Surface Interval: If you have been diving, the recommended practice is to wait 24 hours after your last dive before you can fly, so take this into account when booking flights. You therefore won't be able to dive on your last day (you can see the Komodo dragons instead!).

Luggage: Budget airlines such as Wings Air only allow for 10kg of luggage. Garuda Indonesia offers up to 20kg of luggage. (Not that you'll need much when you're on the islands apart from a few pairs of swimming costumes and sun cream).

Phone Signal: Komodo National Park is very remote so don't expect your mobile to pick up phone signal or Internet connection. Think of it as a digital detox!

When to go: You can visit Komodo Islands from April to December - the dry season. July and August is the peak season so you might want to go outside of this period (although we went in August and it was fine).

Accommodation

Liveaboard

The best way to experience and enjoy the wonderful Komodo National Park is to explore by boat. 'Liveaboard' is literally how it sounds; you sleep, wash and eat on the boat as well as using it as a base for diving or snorkelling escapades. As there are so many remote islands in the national park, being on a boat allows you to spend more time travelling to these distant and untouched areas. I always say that my Komodo Islands liveaboard trip has been one of the most memorable travel experiences I've had in Asia.

Wunderpus Liveaboard

A group of six of us were looking to privately charter a small liveaboard boat that fit within our budget for an August diving trip. We went with the wonderful *Wunderpus Liveaboard* company that is based in the Komodo National Park. The communication and professionalism of one of the founders,

↖ wunderpusliveaboard.com

✉ info@wunderpusliveaboard.com

◎ @wunderpus_liveaboard

$ $590 per person including all meals and diving on Mimic for 4 days + 3 nights. Rates for Wunderpus Phinisi liveaboard start at $300 per day.

Chris (an ex-management consultant from the US), was beyond our expectations and he helped us to create such a fantastic trip. They do have a more luxurious 25m traditional Phinisi boat with private cabins and aircon called *Wunderpus*, but we went for their budget option, *Mimic*. If the idea of sleeping on the deck of a boat with close friends (basically a far-flung sleepover!) in the middle of the Flores Sea in East Indonesia sounds like fun then this trip is for you. The four-day, three-night trip costs around $600 per person, and that includes all diving equipment and at least nine dives, conducted in a group of no more than four divers per guide. The price also includes the tasty meals on board and dragon trekking is also part of the package.

Rascal

If you have cash to splash, have a look at *Rascal*, a super stylish 31m Phinisi boat that's run by my friend Erik, with gorgeous US Hamptons style interior designed by my talented friend Chloe (@paradiseroaddesigns).

 rascal-charters.com

 @rascal_voyages

Hotels

If you do prefer to stay on land, you can look at the following resorts:

Komodo Resort

Located on Sebayur Island, *Komodo Resort* is geared towards divers and comprises of 16 seafront bungalows along with a bamboo restaurant serving seafood and Italian cuisine and a spa offering Javanese massages.

komodoresort.com

From $175 per person/ night full board. Diving and equipment rental is additional.

Plataran Komodo Beach Resort

Located on Waecicu Beach on the island of Flores, this peaceful resort provides a range of activities from yoga to kayaking, cooking lessons to fishing.

plataran.com

From $380 per room/night

Places of Interest

1 Crystal Bay

A stunning stop-off during our trip around the Komodo Islands was the calm waters of Crystal Bay, which, as the name suggests, was a gorgeous bay with sparkling azure water. We took a break from our scuba gear and explored the cove with snorkels. It was also a lovely backdrop for lunch.

2 Pulau Karangan

A small sandbank near the island of Komodo, Pulau Karangan is a picture-postcard tiny island. We hopped off our boat and floundered around in the shallow aquamarine water surrounding this sandy sanctuary.

③ Pulau Kalong

An interesting activity is to watch the spectacular evening event at Pulau Kalong, or 'Bat Island', where you'll view thousands of fruit bats who inhabit the mangrove forest theatrically fly out from the trees and towards the bigger islands for their feed. This marvel occurs at around sunset, and is only observable by boat.

Gili Lawa Darat

 Panoramic Trek

As well as a wonderful underwater world, the Komodo National Park also has fabulous dramatic landscapes to enjoy by foot. There's a nice little trek and viewpoint at Gili Lawa Darat. You hop off at the beach and start on a fairly steep, rocky path (note, it can be slippery so remember to bring a pair of trainers). Huffing and puffing up the hill, you will soon be rewarded with the most stunning scenes of the surrounding islands. We timed our trip for sunset, where we saw a pearly pink sky reflecting on the shimmering sea. Bring a few beers along with you, to crack open at the top of the viewpoint, while enjoying the dramatic scenery of this slice of East Indonesia.

Rinca

 Komodo Dragon Territory

There are around 5,700 giant lizards, or 'Komodo dragons' that live on the islands of Komodo, Rinca and Gili Motang in the Komodo National Park, being the only region in the world to see this ancient species that have roamed here for millions of years. Reaching 10ft in length, these scaly carnivores are known as vicious predators, eating other animals such as deer and goat. We did a short-guided trek on Rinca to see these unique creatures close up. The dragons are generally shy, but do ensure that you're with an experienced guide that can ward off any advances. Be sure to watch the thrilling Komodo fight clip on BBC's Planet Earth II, 'Islands' episode with Sir David Attenborough to get you excited for your own Komodo dragon sighting.

Dive Sites

6 Mawan Island

The icing on the cake of our Komodo Islands trip was our diving session at Mawan Island. We saw the most magical performance from manta rays that were here to visit the 'cleaning station', a location where they come to get their skin cleaned by smaller fish. At only five metres deep, the light was spectacular and it truly felt like we were experiencing a nautical theatre show as the manta rays danced gracefully above our heads.

7 Tatawa Besar

I initially felt nervous about the idea of a 'drift dive', where you allow the ocean's current to transport you, instead of actively swimming yourself. After overusing the oxygen in my tank, I started to chill out and enjoy the natural ride of the current. We saw wonderful whitetip reef sharks as well as cuttlefish, fusiliers, and sweetlips.

8 Batu Bolong

You know you've reached the dive site at Batu Bolong when you see a peculiar hollow rock formation (Bolong means 'hole' in Indonesian). After an early wake-up call, we ventured to the site for a 6.30am dive where we were greeted by a Hawksbill turtle swimming on the surface. We were rewarded with our timing, seeing an array of marine life, including tuna fish, giant trevally, manta shrimp, Napoleon wrasse, fusilier fish and lionfish swimming around the sloping coral wall.

Bianca Todorov

Growing up between Papua New Guinea and Australia, Bianca Todorov was inspired by the natural beauty and art that surrounded her. While living in Wewak on the Sepik River, with her family, she slowly started collecting beautiful items from the Papua people such as wild boar tusks and ancient shell money. In Ubud, these two Oceanic worlds collided; fusing the workmanship of local silversmiths in Bali with the one-off tribal adornments from Papua, *Ewa Tribal Jewelry* was born.

The Jewellery Designer

An Interview with Bianca Todorov

Can you tell me about your background; where are you from and where have you lived?

I was born in Melbourne, Australia. My mother is Dutch-Indonesian and my father is Bulgarian. He became an alluvial gold miner and we ended up in Papua New Guinea for his projects, which is where I grew up as a child. When I was old enough I went back to Australia to do my own thing, but I was always coming back to Papua New Guinea to see my parents, where we would go venturing to the villages. A big chunk of my life has been spent in Papua New Guinea, so that's how it all began.

Back then there was an expat community, and those communities were always social with each other, but my parents were always very different. They employed a lot of the local people and really looked after them and we became like a family. We lived in a town called Wewak, which is the gateway to the Sepik River. The river has about 200 villages that are speckled along it, and that's where all this art in the shop (*Ewa Oceanic Art Gallery*) is from. My mother and I used to buy the adornments such as the tusks and the teeth from the tribes people.

When we went back to Australia, people would ask us what we were wearing! It was just a progression of living amongst people and really liking what they do and wanting to translate that. We really admire the people as artists and craftsmen; what they can create from nothing is incredible. The organic pieces that we use in our jewellery, they have literally hand-carved those with slices of bamboo and then passed those pieces down through generations. When you wear something that is old and handled, it has its own energy.

Can you tell me about your brand *Ewa Tribal Jewelry*, what is the story and inspiration behind it?

Being in Bali, especially Ubud, everything is about silver making. We had a collection of boar tusks and we thought, hey, let's start to play around with this. We came across this amazing silversmith who really understood how to work with organic material. We all connected and thought let's give this ago. And that's how we started designing and turning the tusks and shells into something different. Of course it's not everybody's cup of tea, because it is quite raw. People either like it or they don't – it's a very defined thing. The pieces really are one of a kind. They are hand-crafted and we try to work with 22K gold and high-grade silver.

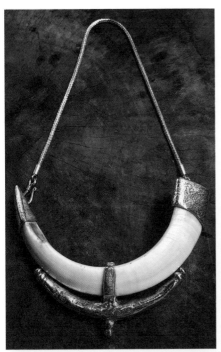

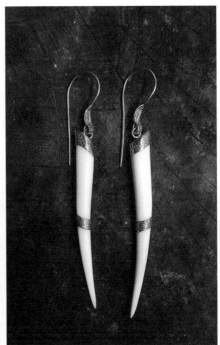

The tribal jewellery is very symbolic - can you explain the significance behind the pieces?

The boar tusks are used as protection, and the tribes people will often use it in their art as well as wearing it themselves. The largest ones are really important; for them it becomes a sign of wealth. The shells are currency, it's bride price – it can be for a dowry, it can be for land, or for an exchange between villages. These important pieces are stored away in houses until they need to be used. They can each be hundreds of years old. There are also shells, not from the beach, but from the mountain. It's like a fossil. They hand carve them further down to give them a symmetrical shape.

When you were creating your brand, how important was it for you to bring Papua heritage into your concept?

It was very important. It's a little bit hard conveying the tribal side, which is quite masculine and raw, and then trying to relate it into jewellery. I have to keep femininity in there, and for women to understand that side of it, but then at the same time I also want them to know where it has come from, and I don't want to dilute it too much. But people are looking for something different. I find it really important that the Papua New Guinea element and the people themselves stay within the brand.

That branding grows all the time, I do it all myself, the photography, the website. I am a fashion photographer by trade. When I was 20, I started working with modelling agencies in Australia, where I was one of the first female photographers to come on the scene. They gave me all the young models, as the younger girls felt comfortable with another girl. I've been shooting ever since then. I'm hoping to go even rawer with the branding and photography.

Can you tell me more about your experience working with the artisans in Bali?

You have to find somebody that you connect with and who understands your vision. We were so incredibly lucky to find the Balinese guy that we now work with. We don't want to be bossy 'bulehs' (*Indonesian word for a European foreigner*) as they call them here. We like him to go off and be able to create as he does. The jewellery is a mixture of his fine delicate work that really matches with the organic pieces from Papua. When working with the silver he can go a bit more hardcore; our silver is rugged and raw, hand beaten, and imperfect. We like everything to be imperfect, we don't want perfect. That's actually one of our things, because everything now is so mass-produced and so mainstream, so we thought, let's go the other way.

What are some of your favourite pieces from your collection?

I wear the half-moon everyday. The Papua New Guinea people will break the shell and create a half-moon, and then they will use it in their own decoration, so this could be in the jewellery for themselves, in adornments, in their skirts, or in special items that they will wear. It's an important piece for them; they will hold onto it and give it to the next generation. We make small collections of these pieces.

Can you explain more about the sourcing of the antique pieces from Papua that go into your jewellery?

We started collecting the pieces 30 years ago. The thing is, there are a finite number of the organic items from Papua. This is not something that we can keep doing and mass-producing in any way. Really, our first collection was revealing it to the market and showing what we do but in the future, the pieces are going to get more precious, especially the gold ones. We can't go back into Papua New Guinea and say 'oh can I have 100 of those shells', because we've been collecting them slowly over the years. For example, the size of these tusks, we'll probably never get them again. That's the hard part about it, once they're gone their gone. We're starting to work even more with silver now, just to have a bit of diversity.

How did you end up moving to Bali?

That just happened. I came here as a tourist and I saw a sign on a door that said, 'family wanted to teach underprivileged Balinese children', and I thought, I want to do that, I'd love to do something here where I'm not a tourist. So my guy and I, we just went, let's go and meet these people. They were an American family and they said we'd really love you to take over our school. We weren't teachers, but we thought, let's give this a go and try it for a month. And those months turned into two and then info four and then six, and two years later we were still doing it. That was nine and a half years ago. We had 60 children, which turned into 200. We had so many children coming to these free English classes every day, that soon we became overwhelmed; it became so much. We started to recruit volunteers so we could step aside.

I had to go back to work and keep doing what I had to do. My guy took it on and helped the school become independent. Our Balinese friends now use that model to create their own schools. That kept us here and one day I saw this little shop in Ubud, and I rang my parents and said, I think I've found a place that can be our gallery, and that's how it all began. Our family has collected everything in this shop, directly with the Papua people. We've met some really amazing people over the years. Sometimes I get so attached to the pieces that we sell in the gallery, I have to hide things out the back! But there are also such lovely people so I know that they have gone to a good home.

What do you love most about Bali?

I'm probably saying what everyone says, but for me it's the people, I'm here because of the people. I come from two of the most beautiful and pristine places on earth; Australia and Papua New Guinea, where I grew up in nature, swimming in amazing crystal clear waters. Here in Bali, the people are what make it. I can't have a miserable day here, because I get on my motorbike and somebody smiles at me - I can never be in a bad mood. I've loved every day for the last 10 years, being in their world. They've helped me become the person I am today, and it's nice to be in a place where being gentle is nice, and being kind and gentle works. Living in Bali will always be the best things I have ever done.

ewatribaljewelry.com

Jalan Dewi Sita 1, Ubud

@ewajewelry

See page 113

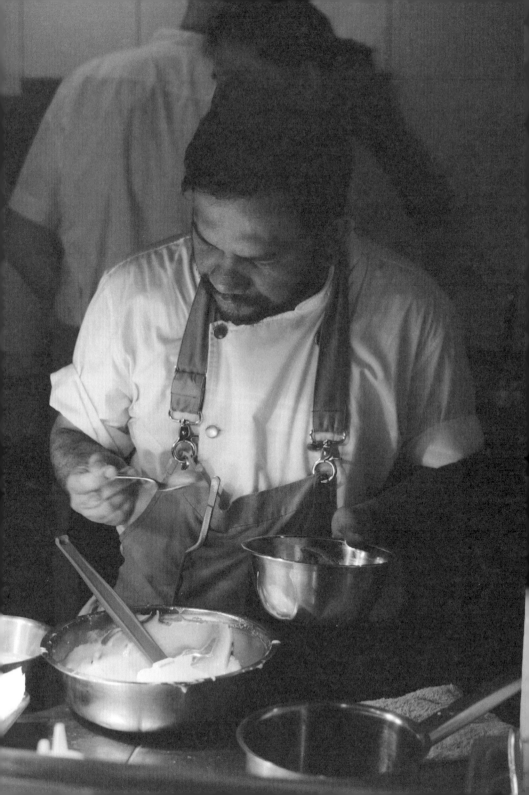

Ray Adriansyah

Alongside Chef Eelke Plasmeijer and restaurant manager Adi Karmayasa, Jakartan born Ray Adriansyah opened *Locavore* in the heart of Ubud town. With a focus on using home-grown ingredients and creating strong relationships with local producers, *Locavore* is considered by many to be one of Indonesia's best restaurants. But these guys are just getting started. After research trips to far-flung parts of the archipelago, they founded *Nusantara*, bringing authentic Indonesian dishes discovered on their travels to a new audience.

The Chef

An Interview with Ray Adriansyah

Tell me about your background; where are you from and how did you get started on your food journey?

I was born and raised in Jakarta, but my parents are originally from Sumatra. I also lived in New Zealand for 10 years; I originally went to do a business course, which was sort of my parent's idea. Back in the day, especially growing up in Jakarta, parents had a big influence over your life. After convincing my Mum and Dad, I eventually went to culinary school.

I first met Eelke around nine years ago and we've been working together ever since. We met in Jakarta when I was applying for a job where Eelke was the head chef, at a restaurant called *Shy*. The restaurant just didn't work; the appreciation of the food back then was just really low for what we did. We did fine dining but we didn't use any local ingredients at all, like all Jakartan restaurants back then. That was crazy; sourcing from France, Japan, Australia, you name it. We stayed there for six months and then we took off to Bali. We started off in Tuban, in a small stand-alone restaurant with 11 villas, where we worked for a year and a half. We then left to go and work for the hotel *Alila Ubud* for almost two and a half years. Then we thought – why don't we open up our own place?

What inspired you to do the 'locavore' concept, using only locally-grown ingredients?

For Elke and I, we sort of did it organically. For us, it made sense that we use local produce instead of importing from Australia or wherever. Especially being in Indonesia where you are surrounded by all these great ingredients. We were also frustrated with the standard of the imported products, which is one of the reasons why we made the shift to local ingredients.

When we were starting out, the consistency of the quality of the imported produce wasn't good at all. Then our suppliers in Bali took us to their gardens and showed us that you can grow almost anything here - beetroot, radishes and strawberries all grow beautifully up in the mountains just 20 minutes from Ubud, so why import from different parts of the world?

For the first couple of years we had two vegetable gardens, but after a while we decided to close those down because it didn't really work. We had a long dry season and that was tough. So then we switched and now we use more local vegetables. We stopped using fennel, strawberries, radishes, and asparagus. Now we do more fern tips, cassava leaves and chayote, which is actually originally from Mexico, but that's what my grandparents used to eat (in Sumatra). I never had any asparagus or fennel when I was growing up as a kid; it makes sense to use these local vegetables, as they can grow naturally on the land in the area.

Nusantara

Jalan–Jalan Project

Can you tell me more about the sourcing of your ingredients within Indonesia – what have been some of the main challenges and memorable experiences?

We focus on sourcing our ingredients in Bali; I would say that 80% of our produce is from here – all the vegetables, all the flowers. For our pork, we use the black Balinese pig, known locally as the heritage animal. We source the rest of our ingredients from other areas in Indonesia, such as Lombok, where we get seaweed and seafood, and scallop when it's in season. We'll also go to Java and Sumatra and we have a couple of shipments from Papua for crabs, which are very nice. The whole local idea is that we use all the produce found around Indonesia. For me that's important.

Finding new ingredients can be hard sometimes. It took us a while to find lamb from Java, and it's actually more expensive than getting lamb from New Zealand and importing it. Finding the suppliers who are keen on what we are doing is challenging, as they normally grow the vegetables that the markets need. So sometimes we do take things into our own hands.

Locavore

I've just been to Cirebon, which is in West Java, where they have super nice mangos. Adi recently went to Lake Toba and found amazing cray fish and aji limo peppers. Eelke is going to Makassar in Sulawesi, which is rich in seafood and has a lot of spices and new ingredients. Going to local markets is always special. For example, a local market in Medan is totally different to a local market in Bali. It's so nice to see new things.

What are some of your favourite local ingredients that we might find in your kitchen in Bali?

I particularly like kemangi, also known as lemon basil, and aji limo peppers, which are found in Northern Sumatra and are similar to citron peppers. I like all of the spices, especially the different asam, also known as tamarind. We are lucky to be in Bali, and to be in Indonesia with all these beautiful products; vegetables and spices especially. The herbs and fruit; they're amazing, especially the mangos and mangosteens, which are in season right now.

What does 'Nusantara' mean and what is the idea behind this restaurant?

The name of the restaurant, *Nusantara*, means 'archipelago' in Indonesian. The restaurant is casual and family-style, with sharing a-la-carte dishes. We try and make it as authentic as possible. This means no recipe changes and no adjustments. If the dish is meant to be spicy then we have to keep it as it is, so we don't reduce the amount of chilli and we don't reduce the spices. That's the whole idea. The restaurant is run by our sous-chef Putu Dodik who has been with us since the beginning. He was the sous-chef at *Locavore* and was up to the challenge, so now he's running it.

Can you tell me more about the research process that goes into the recipes and concepts for your restaurants?

We have a research programme called the 'Jalan-Jalan Project' which takes us to numerous parts of Indonesia. Every month we go to a different city or province and look for original cooking techniques as well as new ingredients. At the same time we also like to make new friends, which helps us to form a fresh context that we can bring back to the restaurants.

I am always curious about Sumatra, which is the island that my parents are originally from. 95% of our staff are Indonesian, so we know where to go. We know that Jogja (Yogyakarta) is famous for its jackfruit dishes, and the food there tends to be sweeter. And we know that Sumatra is great for spices. Being Indonesian, we like our food.

We'll get a mix of members from our team to go on the trips, one from *Locavore*, one from *Nusantara* and one from R&D. We have a test kitchen, which we call the *Local Lab*. The idea for this is that we play around and move things forward, doing a 'work in progress' dinner once a week. So for example, during the week they play around on new ideas, and then on Saturday they can put it into a five or seven-course dinner. This will lead onto new dishes that will be on the menu in the restaurants.

Locavore is modern cuisine – what made you want to start a restaurant, *Nusantara*, using traditional Indonesian flavours?

In Bali, there aren't many Indonesian restaurants. While there are plenty of Balinese restaurants serving nasi goreng or western restaurants doing pasta, there isn't much Indonesian food. Both Eelke and I like our street food. For us it's very authentic. For *Nusantara*, we took this idea and put it into a better location with a comfortable environment with a good kitchen and nice setting. Normally people don't know where to go; they want to eat satay ayam (chicken satay), and they end up in the hotel, which is not very authentic at all – it's just fancy. This is one of the reasons that we opened *Nusantara*, to share those experiences.

What sort of food do you most enjoy eating on your day off?

That's easy. I like my Padang food, Sumatran food. A lot of curries, a lot of chilies.

How important is sustainability when it comes to food and running restaurants?

For us we didn't open *Locavore* or the other outlets to be sustainable, for us it just happens organically. For example employing 95% locals, you are very much being part of the community. When I mentioned that 95% of our staff are locals, 80% are from Bali, mainly from around Ubud. We had a guy who used to work at a garage and now he's running one of our outlets, *Locavore to Go*. One guy used to work at Pizza Hut, and now he's running one of our outlets, so I think that's really cool. Of course there's the importance of where the food comes from as well. I don't think it needs to come from very far away. It doesn't make any sense to order kilos of passionfruit from wherever in plastic, or already pureed.

It is hard work. It took us almost three and a half years to set it all up, to set up the supply chain, to do the 'Jalan-Jalan Project', to do the sourcing of ingredients in different islands, switching from imported seeds to indigenous plants. It took us a while to be able to stop using the big suppliers and go with local farmers. We have five or six vegetable suppliers, three or four fish suppliers, one guy only doing bebeks (ducks). We don't have purchasing, so the boys themselves are responsible for calling, talking to suppliers, chasing them, and handing over the list of ingredients. I did it for the first year, but now the boys do it. There are a lot of things to do. It's a lot of work. There were a lot of frustrations at the beginning. But it is what it is. We just have to do it.

What do you love most about Bali?

The landscape of course – I come from the big city (Jakarta). For Eelke, he likes the people. It's a bit more chilled here than in Jakarta, much less traffic for one. On my day off I can chill out, go to the beach with my little kid. The people who come here are open-minded; the level of appreciation for what we are doing is very high, which of course means high expectations for us.

Ray, Eelke and Adi

locavore.co.id

Jalan Dewisita, Ubud

@restaurantlocavore,
@restaurantnusantara

See pages 108 & 109

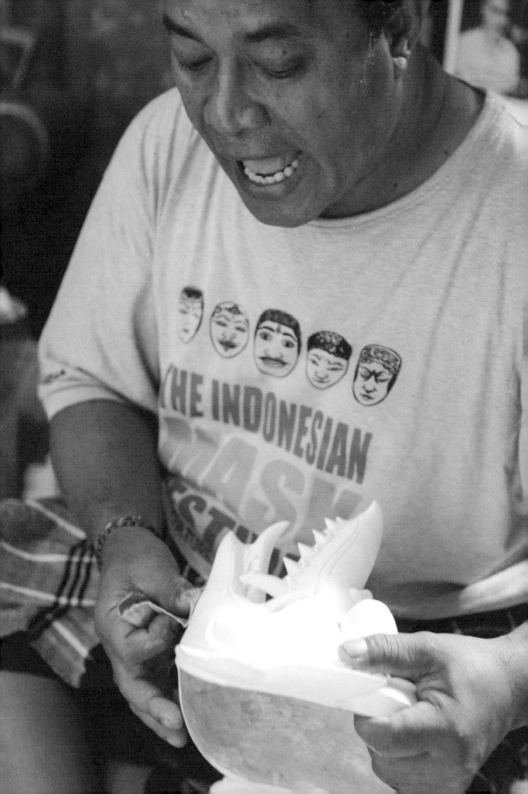

I Wayan Muka

I Wayan Muka comes from a long line of mask makers, or 'Pemahat Topeng' in Indonesian, a skill that has been passed down through generations, and which he has since passed down to his own sons. Located in the centre of the mask making community, Mas, near Ubud, Wayan dedicates his days to producing mythical masks inspired by Hindu tales. As well as creating the masks, the profession also requires performances, which are carried out during ceremonies in the temples.

The Mask Maker

An Interview with I Wayan Muka

The village of Mas, just south of Ubud, is known for its creative industries of highly respected wood carvers and sculptors, including the fascinating mask making community. Indonesia has a long and rich history with masks, known as 'Topeng', and different regions and islands across the archipelago all have their own type of mask variety. In Bali specifically, mask ceremonies have been performed for hundreds of years, communicating ancient Hindu stories.

"Some scholars trace the first known origin of Topeng back to the copperplate charter Prasasti Bebetin dated AD 896 inscribed during the reign of King Ugrasena of Bedulu kingdom. The charter identifies the word pertapukan as the masked dancer, along with a list of artists of the courts, servants, functionaries and even juru jalir – a prostitute. Prapanca's Negara Kertagama, the most authoritative book from the fourteenth century on the leadership of the Majapahit kingdom, describes how King Hayam Wuruk and his queen performed a masked dance story from the Panji cycle."

– Rubin, Leon and Sedana, I Nyoman
(2007) *Performance in Bali*

I went to visit I Wayan Muka at his home in Mas. He lives with his family in a traditional Balinese compound where he runs his small open-air workshop and an enchanting gallery displaying his beautiful mask creations. Like most other 'Pemahat Topeng' (mask carvers), he is both a mask maker and performer. His grandfather was a master carver and dedicated himself to the craft, and the family tradition continued.

'My father did the performing and my mother's specialty was dancing too; she did Gambuh, welcome dancing. It's going down through the generations. I have three children, a son who's 30, a daughter who's 27, and another son who's 25. My sons do the mask carving and performances. Downstairs (in the workshop) *is my youngest son.'*

Wayan leads me upstairs to his gallery. Every inch of the walls is decorated with displays of vibrant and enthralling masks. They seem to stare intriguingly at me – like they're alive, a testament to the ability of the carver.

Each mask has its own character and emotion. There's a green Garuda mask with sharp white fangs and startling burnt-orange eyes and pointed pricked ears. There's a calm-looking queen mask wearing a decorative gold crown, with a gentle red smile and kind eyes.

Hanging from the ceiling is a fearsome Barong mask with a thick long main of hair. A lion-like creature who is known as the king of the sprits, the Barong mask is the most elaborate and takes the most time to produce, featuring rich gold paint and mirror adornments to create an embellished crown. Additionally, the mask has real course animal hairs carefully attached, adding to its animalistic presence.

Wayan explains to me how the masks are cleverly carved to be in the same proportions of an actual human face.

He points to his own face, '*I'll show you; 18 and 15 centimeters*' (he refers to the length and width of his face). '*four, three and four centimeters*' (the length of the forehead, nose and mouth). '*The proportions of my face are the same as the masks. Everyone has this, Balinese or foreigners. If you do five, five, five centimeters then you have a problem when you put the mask on, you can't see out of the eyes, and you have problems with the nose.*'

He goes on to explain further about the creation of the masks. '*This is a process of carving but it's a process of the painting too. There are 75 coats of paint and it takes 10 days to finish a traditional mask from carving to finish. If you do one small mess you have to start again. Each time I put on a coat of paint, I then put the mask out in the sun to dry and then do more painting. After 10 coats of paint I'll sandpaper the mask, then add more colour. If it is raining too much then there will be a problem with the paint as it's no good for drying.*'

Wayan talks about the significance of the wood used for the masks. '*This is special traditional wood from Bali used for masks named 'kaya pule'. This wood has spirit and a power in Hindu. Many Hindu people who make Barong and Rangda* (types of mask) *only use this type of kaya pule wood in the temple, because it has a spirit in Hindu.*'

He tells me when the mask performances tend to take place; '*It's a good day in Bali if there is a full moon, or black moon; it's a special spirit day. At the moment, in August and September, it is cremation period so there are no ceremonies. They will start again in October.*'

Mask makers are also mask performers, and Wayan kindly offers to give me a small show in his gallery. He fixes the mask of 'Topeng Dalam' (the King) to his face, floats out his arms and wiggles his fingers excitedly. He continues with fast, sharp movements of his arms and hands. His head tilts quickly and his whole body and soul becomes the character of the mystical mask. Wayan then puts on the mask of 'Sidakarya', the grinning white face with thick eyebrows and matching moustache, and prominent top teeth. He slowly lets out an evil, almost echoing cackle from behind the disguise. The movements are similar to that of a puppet, which are also famous in the Balinese culture.

I asked him how he felt when he was performing. '*With all the different masks, I have different feelings. Queen, I make a small character, King I make a small and calm character. When I'm doing the Prime Minister I feel strong. Old Man, I feel like an old man. The mask and the feeling are together.*'

We went downstairs to the workshop; Wayan shows me a work in progress piece of a Garuda mask. It has been carved and painted white, and was undergoing a further round of sanding to smooth out the eye sockets. '*I make the wood down here using kaya pule. My family helps me carve and then I'll do the painting. Today we're doing Garuda and Hanuman.*'

Wayan's 25-year-old son was sitting with his legs crossed on the rattan mat in the workshop, holding a special woodcarving knife and working on a carving of a Hanuman mask, which is the Hindi monkey god and a central character in the epic of 'Ramayana'. '*The Ramayana is the same story as Romeo and Juliet,*' Wayan informs me.

The workshop is part of the compound of his family home, filled with pots of paintbrushes and tins of paints, and framed photos of important past mask performances over his career.

In another corner are stacks of tools, knives and hammers, with woodcarvings and chips scattered on the mats. There's a large mask of Rangda, the witch Queen, with a huge volume of blond animal hair fixed to it, and a long ornate gold tongue spilling out from its pink mouth, framed with white fanged teeth.

Topeng Dalam (King)

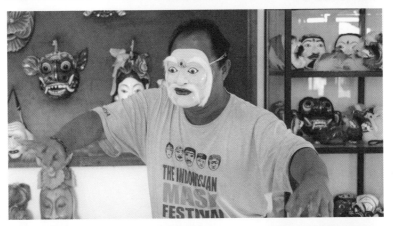

Old Man

Sidakarya

I asked him how important the mask performances were to Balinese culture.

'The mask dance needs to be performed when there is a big ceremony. If there is no mask dancing, then the ceremony can't be completed. That's how important it is to Balinese culture. This is where Sidakerya comes in. He is responsible for performing and ending the ceremony. For Balinese people, Topeng dancing is contact with the spirits.'

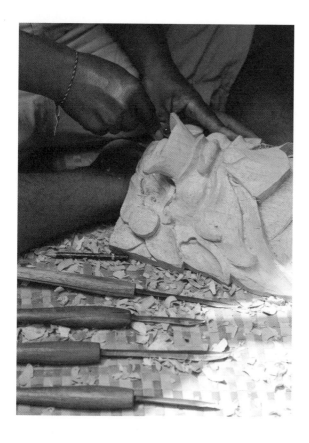

🏠 Batanancak, Mas, Ubud

✉ spiritofmask@yahoo.com

See page 128

My Bali & Islands Travel Notes

Date   Location   Notes

Acknowledgements

The first edition of this book was brought to life through a crowdfunding campaign, with a wonderful group of supporters pre-ordering the book. This second edition was made possible due to the lovely people who bought the book, the shops that stocked it, as well as the folks who helped to me to spread the word about **Lost Guides**.

Thank you to all those that joined me on the exploration side of the project, as well as those that gave me their tips and shared their secrets from Indonesia with me.

Additional photography:

Anna Chittenden profile – Katie McKnoulty
Morning Light Yoga
The Cashew Tree
Mick's Place
Cuca
Mama San
Merah Putih
Sarong
The Slow
Desa Seni
Hujan Locale

Room 4 Dessert
The Yoga Barn
Hubud – Franz Navarrete
Villa Voyage
Pachamama
Slow Villas
Gili Lawa Darat - A.L Evan Nolan
Rinca - Richard Susanto
Turtle - Sergemi
Ewa Tribal Jewelry
Locavore

References:

Rubin, Leon and Sedana, I Nyoman
(2007) *Performance in Bali*